Inside the Classroom

Other Books in the Beeline Books Imprint

The Publishing Center
How to Create a Successful Publishing Center in
Your School, Church, or Community Group

Write-a-thon
How to Conduct a Writing Marathon in
Your Third-to-Fifth-Grade Class

The Magical Classroom
Exploring Science, Language, and Perception with Children

The Treasured Mailbox
How to Use Authentic Correspondence with Children, K-8

Inside the Classroom

Teaching Kindergarten and First Grade

Bobbi Fisher

Beeline Books
HEINEMANN
Portsmouth, NH

Heinemann
A division of Reed Elsevier, Inc.
361 Hanover Street
Portsmouth, NH 03801-3912
Offices and agents throughout the world

The author and publisher thank those who generously gave permission to reprint borrowed material.

Acknowledgments for borrowed material begin on page 91, which constitutes an extension of the copyright page.

Library of Congress Cataloging-in-Publication Data

Fisher, Bobbi.
    Inside the classroom : teaching kindergarten and first grade /
Bobbi Fisher.
        p.   cm.
    Includes bibliographical references.
    ISBN 0-435-08138-1
    1. Kindergarten—United States.   2. First grade (Education)—
United States.   3. Language arts (Primary)—United States.
I. Title.
LB1205.F57   1996
372.24′1—dc20   96-21842
                                                           CIP

Editor: Carolyn Coman
Production: Melissa L. Inglis
Text design: Jenny Jensen Greenleaf
Cover design: Greta Sibley
Manufacturing: Louise Richardson

Printed in the United States of America on acid-free paper
00 99 98 97   EB   2 3 4 5 6 7 8 9

To Pat Broderick,
with gratitude

Contents

Articles by Topic

Integrating the Curriculum

Preface

This collection of articles derives from the enthusiastic response they have received from teachers at workshops I have given around the country. Very often these comments include requests for copies of articles that are difficult to find or that a particular teacher hasn't seen.

These articles also complement my books, *Joyful Learning: A Whole Language Kindergarten* and *Thinking and Learning Together: Curriculum and Community in a Primary Classroom.* They serve as an introduction to some of the ideas that are discussed in those books in more detail, and cover new topics as well.

I have organized the articles according to grade level because I find that teachers generally prefer to read about the specific grade they teach. Nevertheless, since I believe the articles are useful across grade levels as well, I have also included a list in which the articles are grouped by topic.

Although each grade is unique, many of the concepts and teaching strategies appropriate to one grade can easily be applied to another. Kindergarten and first grade have many similarities in terms of classroom management, organization, and materials: children are engaged in shared literacy, writing, reading, social studies, and science. Teachers of full-day kindergartens can certainly adapt some of the organizational procedures described for first grade. The pace outlined for kindergarten may be appropriate for a first-grade classroom of emergent readers. Many kindergarten children can benefit from some of the strategies described in the first-grade articles.

Most of the pieces in this book first appeared in *Teaching K–8*, a monthly magazine for teachers that publishes articles on current theory and classroom practice. Although they were written as separate articles over an eight-year period, some of the themes are similar. (For example, three articles discuss setting up the room and organizing for the first day of school.) However, each of the articles offers different information or views similar information from a different perspective.

I would like to thank the following people and organizations for giving me permission to reprint articles: Theresa Hardy (Eric Clearing House), Yvonne Sui-Runyan (*The Colorado Communicator*), Lori Mammen (*The Writing Teacher*), and Carol Jenkins (Greater Boston Council, International Reading Association).

A special thank-you to Pat Broderick, editor of *Teaching K–8*, who has continually encouraged me and other classroom teachers to write about what we do in our classrooms. I am deeply appreciative of her support.

The Environment Reflects the Program

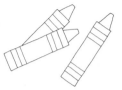

Getting my room ready for a new class of kindergartners is a satisfying and creative time. Every August, I walk into my classroom with renewed excitement and anticipation, remembering what it was like in June, when the children and I "took down the room."

In August, the room seems empty, the cupboard is full, and I again reflect on the goals that guide me in setting up my classroom for a new group of children. Although I'm concerned specifically with setting up a kindergarten, I believe the goals and guidelines I use are appropriate for all primary grades.

I have four goals: first, I want the children to know that they are readers, writers, artists, and mathematicians, and I want them to grow in each of these disciplines; second, I want them to develop as a community of learners in which teachers and children learn from one another in a noncompetitive environment; third, I want them to see learning as whole, integrated and meaningful; and finally, I want them to be involved in making decisions about their own learning.

I also follow some general guidelines I've found to be useful in the past. They are:

- Arrange the room so that children can learn the classroom routine easily and can take care of themselves and their belongings independently.
- Offer a choice of materials that are easily accessible to the children, and, when appropriate, label the shelves and materials.
- Place books and writing materials in each area.
- Start out with a limited number of materials and gradually add new items during the year as the children learn the classroom routines, show interest in various topics, and indicate a need for new challenges.
- Create areas where children can easily display their own work.

Using these goals and guidelines, I start setting up in the room. I know that I want to start with five learning areas—reading, writing, math, art, and dramatic play—plus a snack table and notice board. As the year goes on, new materials will be added to these areas: the puppet theater, water table, and workbench will be introduced and specific curriculum centers will be set up.

Reading Area

Goals

I want to have shared reading every day with the entire class. During independent time, I want the children to read books, listen to story tapes, and use a pointer as they read big books and charts. I want them to read independently, with friends, and with me.

Materials

The carpeted area for shared reading has a teaching easel for big books and for poems, chants, and songs in enlarged text. Shelves are filled with a variety of trade books. In the listening area, there are a tape recorder, earphones, story tapes, and at least four copies of each story-tape text. A comfortable area with pillows and a rocking chair invites independent or paired reading.

Routine

I want the children to come to this area to discover new and familiar texts, and to look forward to gathering for shared reading each morning. Early in the year, I teach the children to use the tape recorder so they can listen to books and record their own stories.

Curriculum

At the beginning of the year I introduce many songs, poems, and chants. I choose those that have been popular in other years, those the children are familiar with, those the children suggest, and my favorites. I also introduce five or six big books during the first two weeks of school. This extensive reading at the start of the year enables the children to achieve early success as readers and leads to more intensive reading.

Writing Area

Goals

I want the children to be engaged in the writing process throughout the year.

Materials

The writing area has a table with six chairs, a desk for quiet work, a large plastic file box for the children's work, and shelves for supplies.

Initially, I place lined and unlined paper, pencils, crayons, and a date stamp on the shelves. Later, I add other kinds of writing paper, construction paper, a stapler, blank books, note paper, envelopes, and the like. The alphabet, in uppercase and lowercase letters, is at eye level and easy for the children to see and touch.

Routine
I start the year with simple rules for writing: draw a picture, write something (which can range from scribbles to sentences), write your name, and record the date with the date stamp. During the first week, I help the children file their work or ask them to place it in the sharing basket.

Curriculum
I want the children to think of themselves as writers, pick their own topics, and take risks as they write.

Math Area
Goals
I want the children to work with a variety of math manipulatives. I also want to offer opportunities for free exploration and directed activities, for individual challenges and cooperative games, and for discussion with peers and teachers.

Materials
Cuisenaire rods are the primary math manipulatives used in my K–5 school. The first day of school, I put them on the math table, inviting free play. Later I introduce pattern blocks, color cubes, Unifix cubes, attribute blocks, chip trading, and so on. Board games, puzzles, Lego and counting pieces, unit blocks, and trucks are always available.

Routine
I want the children to value free play with math materials as an important activity.

Curriculum
At the beginning of the year, I want the children to become very familiar with the materials. I want them to hypothesize on their own, with their peers, and during teacher-led activities.

Art Area

Goals

I want the children to express themselves through a variety of art materials and media.

Materials

Plasticine, recycled materials, and painting easels with poster paint are available. Periodically, I introduce a variety of processes and techniques. Throughout the year we make murals, big books, pop-up books, and similar artifacts.

Routine

I introduce art materials one at a time, so the children can learn how to use them appropriately, as well as how to get them out and put them away.

Curriculum

I want the children to be involved in art as a creative process for self-expression and self-discovery. I want them to integrate art with the literature we read and the thematic environments we study.

Dramatic Play Area

Goals

I want the children to engage in a variety of dramatic play situations and to role-play thematic topics that develop as part of the curriculum. For example, if we are studying pets, we might set up a veterinarian's office in which the children play the roles of vet, secretary, and pet owner.

Materials

My classroom has a loft that I use for dramatic play. At the beginning of the year, it is set up as a housekeeping area. Underneath are a set of big blocks, some large trucks, and a sand table. These environments change throughout the year.

Routine

This area offers opportunities for the children to learn to work cooperatively. Guidelines and rules are agreed on through group discussion, as needs arise.

Curriculum

I encourage free play in this area at the beginning of the year. Sometimes curriculum units grow out of this free play (for example, the children might set up a bank that later develops into a dramatic play environment). Later in the year, I might introduce a unit from our prescribed school curriculum. Sometimes the class might decide on a topic of study as a community.

On the first day of school, I stand at the door and take a last look before meeting the children at the bus. I know I've done everything I can to get the room ready, but it still doesn't look quite right to me. None of the crayons are broken, the trucks are parked in perfect order, and all the sand is still in the sand table. There isn't one child's painting, piece of writing, or block construction on display. I better go and get the kids!

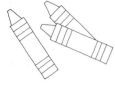

Reading and Writing in a Kindergarten Classroom

- Mandy is a reader. She holds a book in her lap with ease and tells the story in her own way, including much of the language of the text, which she has memorized from hearing it many times. She looks at the pictures and sometimes at me as she reads. Her story is fluent, her voice expressive.
- Sam is another reader. He has also chosen a favorite book, with a simple, familiar text. He reads slowly, focusing word by word, and his voice often lacks expression.
- Allie is a reader, too. Her reading is supported by the meaning of the story, the flow of the language, the pictures, and what she knows about phonics.
- Taisha is a writer. She has just written a grocery list in the house-keeping area. The paper has four lines of scribblelike writing.
- Joey is a writer, too. He has drawn a picture of his house and written random letters (primarily from his name) all over the pages. He has labeled the house H. He reads me his story.
- Stefanie is a writer. She uses many conventions of writing: she leaves spaces between words, spells some words conventionally, applies temporary (invented) spelling in others, uses vowels in every word, and starts two of the three sentences with uppercase letters (Fisher 1991).

Whenever I talk about literacy learning I have to begin with the children and what they can do. When I "kidwatch" (Y. Goodman 1985) as the children read and write, I notice many predictable behaviors that emergent and beginning readers demonstrate. But I also notice that every child is making sense out of print in his or her unique way. My job as a teacher is to help each of them continue to develop as a reader and writer.

Therefore, my definition of reading and writing includes the wide and unique range of reading and writing behaviors demonstrated in my classroom. For example, reading might be reading environmental print, looking at pictures in a book and telling a story, pointing carefully to the print, or beginning to read independently. Writing might be drawing, scribbling, writing random letters, inventing spelling, or beginning to write conventionally. In our classroom, when we refer to reading, the children and I know that we mean using books to create meaning. When we refer to writing, we know that we mean drawing pictures and making letters and letterlike marks.

The Environment
Our classroom is a print-rich environment. Reading and writing materials are easily accessible and can be used throughout the room.

Reading
Big books and charts with poems, songs, and chants in enlarged text are displayed. Fiction and nonfiction trade books, predictable books, dictionaries, and magazines are available on library display shelves, on regular shelves, in plastic bins and crates, and on tables throughout the room. A "listening table" is equipped with a tape recorder, earphones, story tapes, and multiple copies of the accompanying texts.

Writing
The writing area contains a variety of paper, pencils, markers, crayons, rulers, a stapler, and a date stamp and pad. The alphabet, in uppercase and lowercase letters, is hung at eye level, and there are cards with the alphabet and an accompanying picture representing the initial sound of the letter for the children to use wherever they are writing. There is a plastic file crate in which the children file their daily drawings and writing so we have a record of their growth throughout the year.

Conditions of Learning
"To foster emergent reading and writing in particular, whole language teachers attempt to replicate the strategies parents use successfully to stimulate the acquisition of language and the 'natural' acquisition of literacy" (Weaver 1990, p.23). Brian Cambourne (1988) lists these conditions of learning as immersion, demonstration, engagement, expectation, responsibility, use, approximation, and response. In my classroom, I try to create these same conditions to support children's growth and development in reading and writing. I use Don Holdaway's (1979) natural learning classroom model (demonstration, participation, practice/role play, and performance) for organizing the day and planning for groups and individual children.

Demonstration and participation

During group time, which I call shared reading, I give many demonstrations of reading and writing, and the children participate in these literacy experiences by reading along, commenting on concepts of print, and discussing the story. We read many different texts, such as predictable big books, which support emergent and beginning readers, as well as poems, songs and chants, and fiction and nonfiction trade books.

I demonstrate, and the children participate by using a variety of strategies that successful readers use, such as reading the sentence again and using the beginning letter of a word to predict and confirm what it is. We discuss skills in context so the children will be able to use them to create meaning as they read for a variety of purposes. I write in front of the children and they join in, giving suggestions for content and helping spell the words.

All these demonstrations are whole, meaningful, and authentic (K. Goodman 1986). They take place in a noncompetitive atmosphere as each child participates at his or her developmental level. Each child is a member of the literacy club (Smith 1988).

Practice/role play

Choice time follows shared reading. The children have opportunities to practice what they have observed and engaged in during group time. I ask the children to read every day, but I give them lots of choices of what to read. They can read big books, small books, trade books, magazines, or charts or listen to a story tape. They can read alone, with a friend, or to an adult.

I also ask the children to write every day. Usually they can choose their own topic. For example, they can write a book, write with a friend, or write in conjunction with an art project or the developmental play environment that we have set up in the room. The general writing parameters are flexible: draw a picture, write something (this varies from scribbles to labeling to conventional writing, depending on the child's development), date the piece with a date stamp, and write your name.

During choice time, I watch the children and assess what they know so I can help them develop as readers and writers. I listen to them read, or talk with them about their writing. As I get to know them, I am able to encourage learning by taking that teachable moment to support growth.

Performance

To complete the model, children need opportunities to share what they know. In our classroom, sharing takes many forms. Children share their reading by reading to each other or to me and by taking a book home to read to their parents. They share their writing with their peers as they work at the writing table, make a sign for the blocks, or put their piece in the sharing basket. They share with me by coming to show me what they have done, and they share with their parents by taking their work home.

Classroom Goals

My goal for the children in my kindergarten is for them to become independent readers and writers (learners) for a variety of purposes. I want to help each one become a self-motivated, self-directed, self-regulated learner within a community of learners.

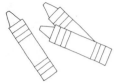

Getting Started with Writing

Organizing the Day

I apply Don Holdaway's natural learning classroom model (demonstration, participation, practice, and performance) to organize the day. At the beginning of the day, the whole class meets for shared reading and writing. During this group time, I demonstrate and the children participate in meaningful, authentic literacy events. For example, we read big books, sing songs, discuss and act out stories, and write a variety of texts.

Choice time follows. The children practice what they are learning in reading, writing, math, art, science, and social studies. At the end of the day (as well as throughout choice time), they have many opportunities to perform or share what they have done.

The Writing Environment

The writing area in my classroom has a table with six chairs, a desk, labeled shelves holding writing supplies (different kinds and sizes of paper, envelopes, rulers, crayons, pencils, a stapler, and a date stamp and pad), and a plastic file crate with hanging folders in which the children store their work.

The alphabet, in uppercase and lowercase letters, is at eye level on a closet door behind the table. There are aminated alphabet cards, with an accompanying picture relating to each beginning sound, for the children to use at the table. The children are expected to come to the writing area sometime during choice time.

Establishing the Routine

Day 1

I begin to establish the writing routine at the beginning of the school year—on the second day of school, in fact—through a series of demonstrations and minilessons, followed by having the children write at the writing table. During shared reading and writing, I briefly tell the children that every day they are going to be drawing pictures and writing about what interests them.

I ask them to do four things on their paper. I call these things the four steps: draw a picture, write something, write their name on their paper, and stamp the date. If they say they can't write, I tell them to do scribble writing or write some letters or words that they know. I purposely keep the instructions brief and simple so that the children will not be too self-conscious or concerned about "doing it right."

During choice time, I am in the writing area helping them establish the procedure. They put their work in the sharing basket, which is kept on the table, and at night I look at the writing and make notes to help me understand my new students as writers.

Day 2

The next day during group time, I demonstrate the four steps by choosing something that happened to me and then drawing a picture, writing about what happened, writing my name, and stamping the date. I want the children to understand that kindergarten writing can be scribbles, letterlike symbols, random letters, labeling, words, and sentences, so I demonstrate each of these ways as I write.

Again, I spend choice time at the writing table, helping the children with the routine as we refer to my demonstration. I encourage the children to take the piece of writing they create home.

Day 3

The following day, we review the four steps and again focus on the different ways that kindergarten children write. The children recall the different ways by referring to the piece I modeled yesterday. Some children come to the chalkboard to demonstrate.

At the writing table, most of the children are beginning to understand the routine and are helping each other as questions arise. This gives me time to show them how to file their work. As the children finish their writing, they come to me and I write each child's name on a colored hanging file and on a manila folder, which goes in the hanging file and holds their work. I explain that the hanging file always stays in the plastic crate so it will be easy to find, and that the manila file can be taken out as necessary. Each child files the piece written that day.

Day 4

The next day's minilesson concentrates on *ear spelling,* a term the children and I use along with *invented spelling, functional spelling,* or *temporary spelling.* Again, my demonstration relates to the general procedure I'm trying to establish at the writing table.

I draw a rough picture of a topic suggested by one of the children, and together we generate the writing. We start with the message and meaning of what we want to say, and then begin to label, write words, and finally write a sentence. We say the words slowly and decide what sounds we hear and what letters represent those sounds.

I spend choice time talking with the children and listening to what they want to tell me about their work. I also take notes. For example, I write down the subject of the piece, how the child talks to me about it, the coping strategies being used, and any writing conventions I notice. Each child chooses whether to file the piece, put it in the sharing basket, or take it home.

Day 5

I find that although some children can almost always decide on a topic, some need suggestions and help in learning how to generate topics. Therefore, we spend group time generating a list of topics. I write the children's suggestions on a piece of tagboard so we can keep it in class and add to it from time to time. The children help me by using their ear spelling, and I fill in letters so that the list will be written conventionally.

The children work independently at the writing table while I begin to assess each child's letter and sound knowledge. (I have time to assess about four children a day.)

Although informal assessment gives me a lot of information about the children, I want to know specifically which uppercase and lowercase letters each child knows, and the extent of his or her letter-sound correspondence. I use the information to plan minilessons for shared reading and writing and when working with individual children.

Day 6 and beyond

Up to this point, the focus of shared reading and writing has been on procedural demonstrations to help the children establish the classroom routines for writing. With these in place, group time begins to focus on authentic literacy demonstrations that relate to what is happening in the classroom and in the lives of the children.

Throughout the year, I write in front of the children, demonstrating different genres such as stories, science reports, invitations, thank-you notes, lists, and signs. These demonstrations include mini-lessons on specific conventions such as spaces between words, letter-sound correspondence, capital and lowercase letters, punctuation, and left-to-right sweep.

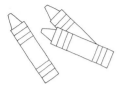

Demonstrations and Minilessons

I use demonstrations to show children how writers construct their texts. During these demonstrations, I give minilessons that focus on using the skills and conventions of print in context to create meaningful texts. Some lessons arise from the comments and questions of the children as we write together as a group. One lesson might be on the use of an uppercase letter at the beginning of a sentence, another on the placement of a question mark at the end of a sentence.

Other lessons are generated by what I notice individual children attending to as I talk with them about their writing—for example, lessons on the use of space between words or on a particular sound the children are using with their "ear spelling." Still others are addressed because, through my teaching experience, I have found them to be developmentally appropriate for kindergarten writers.

I try to write with the entire class every day. Sometimes this writing may be just a few words for a list we are making, while on other days it may be more lengthy, like a story. The four writing experiences that occur and are demonstrated most often through the year in my kindergarten are morning message, letter writing, descriptive sentence, and lists.

Morning Message

Most mornings I post a message on the teaching easel in the group meeting area that tells the children what will happen during the day. They often try to read the message as they gather for the group meeting. We read the message together as we start our day.

Sometimes I write the message in front of the children. This pattern of reading the morning message and then writing one encourages the children to think about writing from the perspectives of both reader and writer. As the year goes on, the extent of their participation deepens.

I start by telling them how I go about writing the message before they come to school. I explain that I look over my plans for the day, and often pick an important event that will happen, because I want them to get excited about the day. If I am not certain about a plan, I let them know so they can anticipate change and look forward to something unexpected.

Once I begin to write, I tell them what I am thinking as I go along. For example, I question myself about how I want to begin. I search for the exact word I want to write, and explain that since I don't want the message to be too long, I have to decide what to include and what to leave out. Soon the children are participating and we are writing the piece together.

Letter Writing

The usual letters that we write in kindergarten are invitations and thank-you notes generated by real situations in the classroom. For example, we invited the school secretary to our classroom to share a song we had written for her son, who was in Saudi Arabia; we also thanked Joe at the supermarket for showing us around on a field trip.

I write on chart paper so that everyone can see the text. After finishing the piece, we decide whether to send it in the enlarged text or to copy it over on letter or note paper. I begin by talking through what I think about as I write a letter, and then ask for specific suggestions, such as how to start, the most important message we want to get across, or which specific closing would be most appropriate.

As the year goes on and we have written several letters as a group, the children participate more quickly and eagerly, and I demonstrate less obviously. The effort becomes more naturally collaborative.

Writing a Sentence

As I confer with the children at the writing area throughout the year, I notice many of them are progressing from labeling their drawings to writing more text. I find that demonstrating the process of moving from labeling to sentence writing helps the children make this change.

One day I told the children how my dog got sprayed by a skunk. When I let the dog in the house, he ran upstairs, jumped on the bed and sat next to my husband, who was asleep. As I told my story, I drew a picture.

Next, I showed them how I could write labels for the dog and my husband, but that I wanted to write some more words to explain what happened. I asked for some ideas from the children, and we agreed on the sentence, "My husband woke up and thought a skunk was sitting by his head." I told the class that, as an author, I could better explain what my husband was thinking by using words rather than pictures.

I talked continuously as I wrote the sentence, asking questions and making comments about letters, words, and spaces between words. We practiced using "ear spelling" and we talked about the letters in the words that we can see but can't hear.

I repeat this general procedure throughout the year, usually with a child's story instead of my own. I spend time talking with the children about their ideas before writing anything, because I want to demonstrate that talking and thinking help us understand our messages better so that we can express them better. Only after a thorough discussion of the substance of the message to be conveyed do we begin to focus on writing skills, conventions, and spelling.

Writing Lists

We are always making lists in my class. We write lists of the characters in a book as we get ready to dramatize a story, the different kinds of boats we know as we prepare to make a boat that floats, and the dramatic play environments we might create. Sometimes I write lists on the chalkboard, and other times I write each item on a separate card so we can sort and categorize them.

In addition to participating in the four different writing demonstrations outlined above, the children see me modeling authentic writing throughout the day. They see me writing notes and lists, keeping records of their learning progress, and writing charts and big books. They also see me make a list of the children I want to read with on a given day, write the weekly news message to parents, and order supplies from a catalog as I ask them to help me with the selections.

The experience of participating in demonstrations during shared reading and observing authentic writing throughout the day helps the children in my class to become engaged as writers.

Sitting in the
Author's Chair

Having an author's chair (Hansen and Graves 1983) is one way to encourage the children to share themselves as writers, to listen as readers, and to experience reading like a writer and writing like a reader.

Sharing is the performance part in Don Holdaway's natural learning classroom model (demonstration, participation, practice, and performance) that I use to organize learning in my kindergarten. As I note in my book *Joyful Learning*, "When the children write for an audience it is important to provide opportunities for them to share their work" (p. 90). Regardless of the manner of sharing, each child should make the choice of *if*, *when*, and *how* they want to share what they have done.

Informal sharing goes on throughout the day as the children talk about their work at the writing table, show it to a teacher or peer, or hang it on a bulletin board in the writing area. Our school library has a shelf where children can leave books that they would like to share with the rest of the school. Children often choose to take their work home to show family members.

If the children want to share their writing with the class, they place it in the sharing basket in the writing area. At the end of choice time, we gather at the rug and the day's leader brings the basket. When we don't have much time, or if the children are having a hard time staying still and paying attention, I hold up each piece and acknowledge the author. Sometimes he or she will read the piece and offer brief comments on it.

Author's Chair

About three times a week, two or three children take turns sharing their writing from the author's chair. I keep a list to make sure that every child who wants to gets an opportunity.

The author sits in front of the group in a special chair labeled *Author's Chair* and shares the piece he or she has written. This might take the form of reading the labels ("I wrote *h* for house"), by slowly reading his or her "ear spelling" word for word, or by giving an oral version of the scribbled writing or the picture.

Next, the author calls on different children to comment on the piece. At the beginning of the year, I ask the audience to start with the phrase "I notice" because this directs them to focus on what the author has done and keeps the remarks positive—for example, "I notice you used different colors," "I notice you wrote a lot of letters," "I notice your dog looks like it's jumping." The author then comments on what has been noticed before calling on someone else.

As the children become risk takers as learners and develop trust in each other, they generate a wider variety of questions and comments. "Why did you draw the horse bigger than than the elephant?" "Why did you decide to write about buried treasure?" "Are you going to change anything in the piece tomorrow?" "I notice a lot of detail in your boat."

Writing Conventions

For the most part, the focus of the author's sharing and the audience's comments are on the picture and content of the work, not on writing conventions. Children are at different levels in their writing development and the power of the piece lies in their ideas and story.

However, sometimes in the introductory sharing, the author mentions a convention he or she has put in. One day, soon after we had discussed that every word has a vowel, Victor commented that he had put a vowel in every word in his piece. As author, he was in charge. Once in a while, someone in the audience notices a convention. Rachel told Stevie, "I notice that you left spaces between the words." Stevie was validated for something he had done. These two kinds of comments had meaning for the authors because they focused on what they knew and could do.

Occasionally a comment, often phrased in the form of a question, can put the author on the spot. When Brian asked, "Why didn't you put an *e* at the end of lov?" Sally didn't know what to say because the question focused on what Brian knew, not what Sally knew. The question didn't come out of Sally's experience or understanding.

Supporting the Children

My role is to support the children in becoming more and more in charge of the author's chair by helping them develop a procedure for sharing and by modeling what writers (the authors) and readers (the audience) do in the process. At the beginning of the year, although I sit in the group as one of the audience, I am more directive about what goes on. As time passes, I become just another member of the group.

During the first few days of author's chair, I initiate the introductory reading by the author, the "I notice" questions, and the procedure for calling on people to share, by sharing a piece I have written. Then, after two children have shared their work, we discuss what went on and begin to write some rules for the audience. We start by focusing on the role of the audience because everyone has participated as a member of that group. The rules usually include, *Don't talk*, *Wait to be called*, and *Say what you notice*.

After a few weeks, when most of the children have sat in the author's chair, we write some rules for the author: *Hold your paper so everyone can see it*, *Don't be silly*, and *Don't call on the same people all of the time*. Throughout the year, we review, edit, and rewrite these rules.

I continually demonstrate different audience responses. At first, I mention things I "notice": "I notice that you have a capital at the beginning of your sentence." Then, when I feel that enough trust has developed in our classroom community, I model more open-ended comments and questions that go beyond what the author is doing: "How did you learn to draw roofs on houses?" "Are you going to draw any more pictures about baseball?"

Throughout the year, during author's chair, we continually focus on both the writer's stance (as an author) and the reader's stance (as an audience member). My goal is for the children to take more and more responsibility in the process and know that they are authors.

Beyond Letter of the Week

Kindergarten teachers often ask me whether it's a good idea to use a letter of the week program. I reply that although I think it is important for children to know letters and sounds, I believe that focusing on one letter at a time for an extended period doesn't support children in their literacy development; that having a letter of the week sends the message that reading and writing is knowing letters and sounds, not the construction of meaning; and that the children's interests, rather than a letter of the alphabet, should direct and guide the curriculum.

Limits of Letter of the Week

For kindergartners, "doing" a letter a week means learning and drilling on a specific letter name and letter sound. By overemphasizing the graphophonemic (letters and sounds) cueing system and thus minimizing semantic (meaning) and syntactic (grammar) strategies, letter of the week conveys some misconceptions about reading and writing: that reading is sounding out; that knowing letters and sounds is a prerequisite to learning to read; that the graphophonemic cueing system is the most important system in learning to read; that each letter is equally important in reading and writing; and that writing is labeling. It suggests a sequential view of reading in which letters are learned first, then sounds, and finally words, which are eventually put into simple sentences.

It also requires that all the children participate in the letter activities. This wastes the time and limits the reading and writing development of those who know the letters or who can already read, and decontextualizes literacy for children entering kindergarten as emergent readers or with limited experience with print.

In order to accommodate a letter of the week program, curriculum tends to focus on contrived topics or isolated subjects (usually picked by the teacher) and is controlled by the weekly time frame rather than by the engagement of the children. Letter of the week directs, and therefore limits, curriculum content and the ways that children and teachers generate curriculum, thus restricting children's development as lifelong learners.

Letters and Sounds Throughout the Day

How then do we help children learn about letters and sounds in a kindergarten that does not do letter of the week? How do we expand the literacy growth of the children who already know letters and sounds or who are reading? How do we generate meaningful curriculum for everyone? The following vignettes describe how children in varying degrees of literacy development interact with letters in meaningful contexts in my kindergarten, and how I respond to and evaluate them during these authentic literacy events.

It is 8:40 and the children begin to enter the classroom. Mary puts a note in the basket telling me that she will be picked up after school. I read it with her and comment that the *M* in Mrs. Fisher starts like her name. Stevie gets his name strip to copy as he signs in. I acknowledge that he is writing a lowercase *e*.

When I start singing "The Wheels on the Bus," the children gather on the rug. Throughout group time, I point to the enlarged texts of songs, poems, and big books. I ask children to raise their hands if they have a *B* at the beginning of their name. Billy and Tom Brown respond. Debby says that she has a *b* within her name. For a minute or two there is chatter about letters in names. The group refocuses as we sing "If I Had a Hammer." I ask the children what they notice and call on individuals so we can all hear what is said. Sam notices the pictures of the hammer and we point to the corresponding word. I ask everyone to count the number of *h*s on the chart. There is silence. I raise my pointer and the children whisper the answer. Then I move it along the text and we say the sound of *h* every time we come to a word beginning with *h* and we say the word.

Someone asks if we will be going outside for recess, and I refer the class to the day's schedule on the board. Ryan has learned to read the schedule. Recess is important to him. We talk about looking for the *r* for recess. Next, the leader for the day picks the big book *The Enormous Watermelon* (Parks & Smith) to read to the class. It's a favorite and we've read it many times. I focus on the title for a few minutes, then ask, "If you were the author, what word could you use instead of *enormous*?" As I write the suggestions on the board, we talk about their meaning and spelling. We decide to read the story substituting the word *gigantic* and I write it on a Post-it, which I move from page to page.

In the writing area, Meagan is saying the alphabet as she points to the letters on the wall. She stops when she gets to *h* and writes it under the house she has drawn on her picture. Then she adds some random letters, and turns to Stephanie to tell her about her new house. Scott asks Dennis if cat begins with *c* or *k*, and Dennis writes a *c* on his paper. Rachel asks me how to spell *walk* and I tell her to write it the best she can on scrap paper before I talk with her about it and give her the conventional spelling.

Several children have returned to the art table for the third day in a row to work on constructing rockets. Yesterday they got some books at the library, and today I plan to read one of them during story time. I hadn't planned that we would study rockets, but I capitalize on these interests generated by the children. They have begun to make a museum of their constructions, complete with labels, and Devon has joined them to make a model of Saturn. I show him a book about the planets and we look for *s* in the index to find the pages for Saturn. We notice that there are a lot of words beginning with *s*.

Explicit Teaching of Letters and Sounds

Although discussions about specific letters and sounds occur throughout the day, I also give explicit instruction about them based on what I know as a teacher about emergent and beginning reading, what I notice children are working to gain control over in their reading and writing, and in response to specific questions they ask.

For example, I notice that Ryan is working with *w* in his writing, both to match the sound to the letter, and to write the letter correctly. Therefore, during shared reading we focus on words beginning with *w* in a text such as *Mrs. Wishy-Washy* (Cowley), and practice tracing the letter in the air or on the rug as I write it on the chalkboard. We also generate a list of *w* words, which I write on a strip of paper, and talk about the children's names with *w*s in them. This explicit instruction is always associated with text. We read the text, focus on a feature of the text (in this case, *w*), examine it, and then read the specific feature again in the original text.

Assessment of Letter and Sound Knowledge

It is important that I know specifically what letters and sounds the children in my class know so I can help them in their literacy development. During the first month of school, I formally evaluate each child, using the letter-identification procedure developed by Marie Clay (1993b). On one form, uppercase and lowercase letters are randomly sequenced on the page. The children tell me the ones they recognize and I record their responses. Sometimes I ask them for the beginning sound of the letter and/or a word that starts with the letter. I administer this same procedure again in March and share with the children and their parents their growth over the year.

I continually assess the children informally throughout the year, observing and recording the letters they use in their writing. These procedures help me plan for both group and individual teaching. They indicate specific letters I may want to make explicit during shared literacy, and identify specific children who may need more support during writing or more time with alphabet books.

In my kindergarten we spend *more* time on letters and sounds than we did years ago when I followed a letter of the week program. We apply letter and sound knowledge strategically as we read and write for meaningful purposes. We integrate the graphophonemic, semantic, and syntactic cueing systems as we learn about the world. The curriculum generates from the authentic interests of the children, not from a letter of the alphabet.

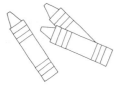

Assessing Emergent and Initial Readers

"I feel that I need to develop a written evaluation profile that accurately and comprehensively demonstrates the progress my children have made in reading and writing," Mary said at a workshop I was giving.

Mary, a first-grade teacher, continually evaluates reading comprehension, assesses reading stages, and monitors the reading and writing skills and strategies her children are using. But, she said, she needed a systematic way to record her observations. "I want to be accountable to myself and the children, as well as to the parents, my principal, school support staff, and other teachers," she explained.

Mary's comments are similar to those of many kindergarten and first-grade teachers with whom I talk. As I share the procedures I use to assess emergent and initial readers in my kindergarten, I encourage teachers to develop their own set of assessments that address their needs as well as the needs of the children and school system.

My assessment framework is organized into three categories: beginning-of-year assessment, ongoing assessment, and end-of-year assessment.

Beginning-of-Year Assessment

During the first two months of school, I conduct a series of assessments with each child. I use these assessments to plan large-group instruction throughout the year and to plan specific support for individual children.

Reading and writing interview

I start by interviewing each child. I tape-record the interview and take notes on a printed questionnaire (Fisher 1991). The questions fall into four categories:

- General interests: "What are some of the things you like to do?"
- The reading and writing environment at home: "Who reads to you at home?"

- General knowledge about reading and writing: "Why do people read and write?"
- The reading and writing process: "When you're reading and come to a word you don't know, what do you do?" (In kindergarten, I ask reading process questions only when I'm interviewing independent readers, but first-grade teachers should include this category with all their students.)

Reading assessment
I observe children "reading" during choice time and/or when I ask them to read to me. On various checksheets and forms, I record

- General observations: interest, enjoyment, concentration.
- Sense of story: telling a story from pictures, retelling a familiar story.
- Conventions of print: book handling, awareness of and attention to print.

Reading stage: I use the Reading Development Continuum in *Reading, Writing and Caring* (Cochrane et al. 1984).

Writing assessment
For this assessment, I make it a point to

- Observe and record writing behavior during writing workshop: handedness, pencil grip, letter formation, concentration, interest, interaction with other children.
- Confer with each child about a piece he or she has selected.
- Assess a piece of writing: drawing, sense of story, spelling stage.

Letter, sound, and word-sound identification
I use the letter-identification procedure developed by Marie Clay (1993b) and record the children's response to

- Letter recognition: uppercase and lowercase letters.
- Sound identification and sound-symbol relationship: beginning consonant sounds. (I sample here rather than deal with every consonant.)
- Word-sound identification: words that begin with a certain letter. (Again, I ask for just a few. First-grade teachers may want to ask for sounds and words for all the letters.)

Ongoing Assessment
The beginning-of-year assessment is the framework for the process-oriented assessment I conduct throughout the year. I continually

	Reading Assessment					Beginning of the year Sept. 6 - Oct. 1	
Key 1. Most of the time 2. Some of the time	General			Sense of story		Concepts about Print	
3. Not noticed yet ✶ very well done + satisfactory o needs time	Interest in books	Enjoy-ment	Concen-tration	Makes up a story	Retells a story	Book handling	Attention to print
André	1	1	2		Hairy Bear ✶		2
Brian	3 doesn't choose						
Cameron	2	2	2	+ very short		Started at back	3
Carol	1	1	1	told long story to a doll	The Red Carpet ✶	✶	1

FIGURE 1   *Reading assessment chart*

observe and assess the children in a wide range of contexts, and adapt instruction to meet their immediate needs. Evaluation and teaching occur simultaneously. Two of the areas I assess are:

- Detailed reading information: reading stage, use of the three cueing systems, current reading interests and books selected for independent reading. About every two weeks, I listen to each child read, and I record the reading stage and the reading strategies being used.
- Detailed writing information: interest in writing and sharing, topic choice, conference notes, developmental spelling stage.

For my ongoing assessment I rely primarily on anecdotal records. I jot down significant incidents that occur during the day, whenever possible noting verbatim what the children say. I record my observations on weekly class lists. Each month, I summarize the information in the children's individual assessment folders and include a current piece of writing.

End-of-Year Assessment
This assessment is similar to the beginning-of-year assessment and follows the same general procedures. I use it for program evaluation, end-of-year parent conferences, and class placement.

Reading and writing interview

In the interview, I focus on what the children can tell me about themselves as readers and writers, and what parts of the reading and writing program have been important to them during the year. One of the questions I ask is, "Did you learn more by reading with a friend or by yourself?" (Fisher 1990).

Reading assessment

My ongoing assessment records give me most of the information I need to complete this section. However, I fill in any missing or incomplete information, and administer the Concepts About Print test in Marie Clay's book (1993b) to children who are still emergent readers.

Writing assessment

In addition to relying on the assessment records I've kept throughout the year, I

- Go over individual writing folders with each child. We sort the pieces according to month, pick favorites for a special portfolio, and celebrate the growth made over the year.
- Complete a written evaluation of a writing sample.
- Ask each child to write a list of all the words he or she can spell. (First-grade teachers may want to include this in their beginning-of-year assessment.)

Letter, sound, and word-sound identification

I assess this both orally and in writing:

- Orally, I test each child's letter knowledge and assess to what degree he or she identifies sounds with letters and words.
- I ask each child to write her or his full name on a blank piece of paper; to write the numerals from 1 to 10; and to identify a simple picture (of a bike, for example) and write the upper- and lowercase letter that begins the word illustrated by the picture.

I saw Mary the other day. She has used some of my suggestions, adapted others from the professional reading she has done, and created strategies of her own. She feels she has developed effective assessment procedures that are organized and documented. Her principal and colleagues are impressed with her procedures and plan to use them to replace some of the standardized and formal testing they have been using.

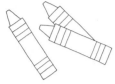

Starting the Year in a First-Grade Classroom

A few weeks before the end of school, a friend called to ask if she could visit my first-grade classroom. She was going to be teaching first grade in the fall after having taught kindergarten for a number of years, and she knew that I had made a similar change the year before. She wanted to see how I set up my room and to talk with me about my daily schedule and how I planned for the beginning of the school year (Fisher 1991).

The Room Arrangement

The physical setup of my classroom reflects what I believe is important about the learning that goes on in it.

Reading area

This area, called "the rug," is where the whole class gathers for community sharing time, shared reading, and student sharing. Books are sorted into cardboard boxes and plastic bins according to categories, and these containers are placed on the floor around the edge of the area. Big books are separated into fiction and nonfiction categories. There are maps of the United States and the world, a calendar, and a chalkboard. A teaching easel, on which I can display charts, plain chart paper, and big books, as the case may be, stands in one corner. Poems and songs are taped to wire hangers and suspended from hooks and nails that the children and I can reach easily.

Writing area

There are four tables in my classroom at which the children do most of their writing and group work. Although each child has a designated seat, they often switch places or work on the floor or at one of the individual desks spread around the room. General supplies (paper, pencils, markers, crayons, date stamp and pad, alphabet strips, scissors, hole punchers, and staplers) are on a shelf. Each child has a cubby to store his or her personal supplies. Writing folders are kept in hanging files.

Art area

The art table, paint easel, and storage shelf are located near the sink. The shelf holds paper, recycled materials, stamps and ink pads, chalk, crayons, Cray-pas, and watercolors.

Science and math area

There are three shelves and a large table in this area. The shelves store math manipulatives (Cuisenaire rods, pattern blocks, attribute blocks, Unifix cubes, number bars, chip trading materials, geoboards, color cubes, calculators), science supplies (empty containers, magnifying glasses, eye droppers), display boxes containing science artifacts and specimens (magnets, wasps and hornets, and items associated with the ocean and the weather), and book boxes categorized according to topic. At the table, the children record their observations, perform experiments, and talk about the ever-changing displays of objects that we all bring in.

Dramatic play area

This area usually reflects what we are doing in social studies, and the setup changes throughout the year—a Japanese home, a television studio, a homestead. Unit blocks are available, and a puppet theater is stored there.

Routines and Procedures

During the first weeks of school, I establish a few important routines and procedures that will encourage my students to make choices, build community, develop independence, and engage with learning throughout the year, and that will provide a framework for the learning atmosphere I want to develop. Predictable procedures allow the children and me to collaborate in planning much of the year's focus and content.

Settling in

The first half hour sets the tone for the rest of the school day. During September, the children learn the general principles of settling in. I want them to establish the routine of taking care of specific custodial duties—signing in, putting school and classroom notices into their school bags to take home, getting their materials ready. I also want them to know that this is a time for them to greet their friends, talk with me, look at things in the science area, and respond to a variety of learning experiences set up around the classroom.

Each morning, on a sheet of paper attached to a clipboard, I write down various things for students to do during this time. I put a star beside the items that they have to do. On the first day, the paper might look like this:

Thursday, September 3, 1992
* 1. Sign in. (Each child writes his or her name on a paper.)
* 2. Put the notice into your bag. (I leave any school or classroom notices on the check-in table.)
  3. Write your name and favorite number on the math chalkboard.

For the first few days, I help the children read the list and complete the tasks. As they begin to establish the routine and figure out the instructions together, I step back and find other things to do. By then I have introduced writing folders and the children have become more familiar with the classroom, so I add other suggestions, such as
* 4. Get your writing folder ready.
  5. Estimate the number of chips in the jar. (The children write their initials and estimate on a piece of paper attached to a clipboard.)

I only star the items that I require each child to do. This keeps this first half hour of the morning relaxed, gives the children choices, and allows them to engage in their own interests.

Writing

At the beginning of the year, I start establishing the writing procedures that will continue and develop throughout the year.

All the children have writing folders, which are stored in plastic hanging files in the writing area. In these folders, they keep ongoing work. As the year progresses their writing folders contain a personal dictionary, "have-a-go" papers (on which they practice the conventional spelling of words they are using), proofreading papers, and other writing assignments.

After the children have had about ten minutes to get settled and talk with their friends about their work, we set the timer for a few minutes of quiet writing, during which we talk only if it is necessary for the progress of the piece being worked on. This helps the children focus for a while, and eliminates some of the distractions that interfere with their concentration.

Writing is followed by an hour of workshop, during which children choose to learn through art, dramatic play, math, reading, social studies, science, and/or writing. On a given day it might look like this: Ian and Tony continue to work on the book they are writing together . . . Heather, Laura, and Ryan read a big book . . . Chelsea, Rachel, and Victor create a story as they build with unit blocks . . . Lindsey and Andy work at the computer . . . Stevie, Aaron, Amy, and Stacey explore finger painting in the art area . . . A.J. and Jennifer record their observations of a wasp's nest, an assignment to be completed during the week . . . Jenna and Junior are in the hall making crayon rubbings of things around the school for a book . . . David, Julianna, and Ellie create a puppet show . . . and James reads to me.

I introduce workshop in September by establishing simple procedures and presenting projects that are familiar to the children from kindergarten. Then I slowly introduce new materials, processes, and possibilities and incorporate the interests and suggestions of the children.

Each Monday, I also introduce assignments that I expect everyone to complete by Friday. These might include things like a science observation, an innovation or extension of a common text we have read as a class, or a new art process such as spatter painting. I limit these assignments so that the children will have plenty of opportunities to make their own choices, and I try to make certain that these all-class projects are meaningful to everyone.

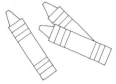

Planning for the First Day of School

Planning for the first day of school is very important to me because I know the first day sets the tone for the entire year. There is only one first day.

As we follow the daily routine, which will remain constant throughout the year (my daily schedule is shown in Figure 1), I'm aware of the following messages about teaching and learning that I want the children to begin to understand:

- We are a learning and caring community.
- We all are writers.
- We express ourselves and understand our world through all the arts, including music, drawing, painting, and drama.
- Science gives us an opening to our world.
- Math is a way of thinking, and we learn both individually and collaboratively.
- Through social studies we learn about ourselves and people throughout the world.
- We all are readers.

8:40 Settling in
9:10 Community circle
We are a learning and caring community.

What I do throughout the day to demonstrate that I care about the children sets the tone for the year. The first morning I stand at the doorway and welcome them individually as they come in. They are then greeted by my assistant, who gives them a name tag and helps them complete a few tasks such as signing in, hanging up their jackets, and finding their writing folder at their table.

When all of the children have arrived and settled in, I move to the rug and begin singing. This is a signal that I use throughout the year for everyone to gather together. The first day, I try to pick a few songs that the children might know, and I invite them to join in. The

8:40	Settling in
9:10	Community circle
	Group meeting
9:45	Writing
10:30	Workshop
11:10	Snack and Recess
11:30	Math
12:15	Inquiry
12:50	Recess and lunch
1:35	Reading
2:20	Specialist
3:00	Ending the day
3:10	Home

FIGURE 1   *First-grade daily schedule*

songs are either written on charts or sung from books. I then read *Brown Bear, Brown Bear, What Do You See?* by Bill Martin, Jr., a familiar book they have probably read in kindergarten.

Then we introduce ourselves, and talk about how we felt before we came to school and how we are feeling now. We briefly discuss the rule *Be kind to each other*, and go around the circle sharing ways we can follow the rule. I jot down the ideas the children come up with. Later, I put the ideas on a chart so that we can refer to them. I also add more ideas as the year goes on.

9:45 Writing
We all are writers.
The children have been sitting for about thirty-five minutes, so the directions I give for writing need to be brief. I tell them that I want them to draw a picture, write about it, put their name on the paper, and stamp the date. I also give them a choice of plain or half-lined paper. Each child then goes to the table where his or her writing folder is and begins.

For the first day of school, I place crayons, pencils, and a date stamp at the tables, but soon the children will be able to get their own materials at the beginning of writing time.

I write along with the children for about five minutes, and then I walk about the classroom, encouraging and acknowledging their work. When they finish, they bring their writing and folder to the rug and look at books while they wait for their classmates to finish.

When everyone has finished and is assembled, we talk briefly about how the writing went. They then put their writing folders in a six-by-twelve-inch (open) plastic file box and their writing in a special basket so I can look over the pieces after school.

10:30 Workshop
We express ourselves and understand our world through all of the arts, including music, drawing, painting, and drama. Science gives us an opening to our world.

Workshop is a time when the children have opportunities to choose what they want to learn and how they want to express this learning. It's also a time for conversation and activity as we integrate and generate curriculum.

On the first day, I put several workshop choices at the tables—watercolors, along with fresh flowers as a suggested topic for a painting; science books and artifacts (a box of magnets, for example); an empty aquarium with a sign in it that asks, "What could live in this?" However, as the year goes on, a combination of teacher and student choices are available.

11:30 Math
Math is a way of thinking, and we learn both individually and collaboratively.

Although math is integrated into much of what we do during the day, we also set aside a time just for math.

The first day I place four kinds of manipulatives—Cuisenaire rods, pattern blocks, Unifix cubes, and number bars—on separate tables and encourage the children to explore them—play with them and build things. As they move from table to table, I observe, take notes and join in from time to time. At the end of this period, we'll talk about what we discovered and liked.

If children knock over each other's buildings or throw blocks, we make some rules and discuss the reasons for them. Thus, our main rule, *Be kind to each other*, begins to include some specific rules as needs arise in the classroom.

12:15 Inquiry
Through social studies, we learn about ourselves and people throughout the world.

Social studies, in the broad definition of learning about ourselves and our world, is integrated into everything we do. It starts in the classroom as we build community by greeting each other, singing and reading together, and sharing our feelings about the new school year; it continues as we write, paint, discover, and build together.

On the first day, however, I also want to launch us into the content of social studies: learning about ourselves in relationship to people and places around the world.

I start by reading Lore Lehr's *A Letter Goes to Sea*, which is the first of many "trips" we will take to places around the world. (You may have trouble locating a copy, but give it a try. Your children will love the book, and so will you.)

The story is about a young boy named Jens, who lives in a lighthouse off the coast of Denmark. On a piece of paper, he draws his picture and writes, "Who will be my friend?"

He puts the note in a bottle, corks it, and throws it into the sea. The bottle comes ashore at various places around the world. Each time the bottle is washed ashore, a child finds it, adds her or his picture and throws it back into the sea. Finally, the bottle returns to Jens, who now knows that "I have friends near and far, black and white."

As I read the book, the children take turns either holding the bottle and passing it to a friend, or pinning a paper bottle on the world map at the locations where the bottle lands.

Our group discussion today introduces a project for tomorrow, when each child will draw his or her picture in a section of a long, accordion-folded sheet of paper. We will create a bulletin board that links us to each other and to children and places around the world through the common experience of a piece of literature.

1:35 Reading
We all are readers.

We do a lot of reading the first day, beginning with shared reading as the children sing and read familiar rhythmic poems and books. Earlier, during morning group, they have learned a simple four-line poem, which I've written on a chart. First, we read it together several times and then I ask for volunteers to read it alone. With each reader, the others become more confident to give it a try. Eventually everyone can read it, either by "reading the words" or from memory. I try to read about seven books to the class on the first day of school, and we start a list of every book that's read aloud during the year.

The children also pick a few books to read independently, and we begin to establish the routines for quiet reading.

3:00 Ending the day

I don't have a specialist on the first day, which gives us time for another story or an extra recess. But before we go home, we return to our community circle and discuss what we liked about the day just ended and what we are looking forward to during the second day of school.

After the children have gone, I reflect on the day and plan for tomorrow. Who needs my special attention tomorrow? What do we need to discuss next in order to keep building community? Were the children comfortable picking their own topics for writing and using invented spelling? Were there enough choices during workshop and what needs to be added tomorrow? Could they handle the free choice during math? What was their engagement during group inquiry? Were they able to look at books quietly for five minutes, and can I extend the time? How can I include in tomorrow's plans what the children said they were looking forward to during the second day of school?

Getting Democracy into First Grade—or Any Grade

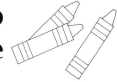

Creating a classroom in which children are authentically engaged in learning and are responsible for establishing and promoting a community of learners is a worthy challenge. Class government helps organize and manage my first-grade classroom (Fisher 1995).

Routine Procedures

Tyler is one of the first children to enter the classroom. He hangs up his coat, signs in on the computer, and goes to his table to see what committee work he has to do. He's on the reading committee, so he checks to see if there are books to be taken back to the library.

Caroline is the moderator for the day, so she starts getting the lunch count ready. Michael notices that we will be having a class meeting in the afternoon, so he writes down a topic for discussion—better ways for everyone to get books for silent reading—and puts it in the suggestion box.

These practices—active committee work, leadership by a student moderator, and regular class meetings—are representative of the democratic procedures that are part of the class government in our first-grade classroom. Everyone is on a committee, the leader for the day is called the moderator, and about twice a month we have a class meeting to discuss classroom issues.

Five Committees

The class is divided into five committees: math, reading, science, trips (social studies), and writing, which correspond with our major disciplines of learning. Membership on a committee lasts about eight weeks.

Tables serve as the main "offices" for committee members. Each table is located near the shelves that hold the supplies related to the committee's discipline and a bulletin board that displays related news and topic projects. A plastic file box, holding the children's writing and workshop folders, and a committee clipboard, listing daily jobs and committee members, are kept on each table.

Math Committee: food pantry, estimating project, announcing the groups, box math.

Reading Committee: organize class reader, take books back to the library, organize books on bookshelf.

Science Committee: plan a class observation, straighten science books, organize displays on science table.

Trips Committee: postcard project, trivia question, pass out passports, straighten the area, recycle paper.

Writing Committee: change the date on the board, change the date stamp, empty the pencil sharpener, clear sharing board, straighten writing shelves, check floors, clap erasers.

FIGURE 1   *Committee jobs*

When the children come in each day, one of their tasks is to check the committee clipboard and perform any committee work necessary to get ready for the day. On a given day, for example, the math committee prepares an estimating project for the class, the reading committee keeps track of the class reader for the day, the science committee plans a class observation, the trips committee adds postcards to our bulletin board, and the writing committee changes the date on the chalkboard and date stamps. Each morning I underline the tasks that need to be done, and add any other special jobs.

In September

When the children arrive on the first day of school, they find their name card at the committee table I have assigned them to. The only thing I'm trying to do at this point is create a balance of boys and girls, but when we change committee assignments throughout the year, the children have some choice. Also, although the children often work at their committee tables, they have many opportunities to choose other places to sit throughout the day.

At an early class meeting, we brainstorm jobs that each committee can do. I type up each committee's jobs, as well as the names of the committee members, so that children can refer to it each day on the clipboard.

One way to keep the work and goals of the committees alive is to change committee membership from time to time. We do this about five times a year, or about every eight weeks. The children write down their first two committee choices and I decide on the final membership. I usually assign five children (sometimes four, sometimes six, depending on the number of students in the class) to a committee.

Each time we change committees, the new members meet to review the jobs. Some of the jobs are standard throughout the year, such as emptying the pencil sharpener, watering the plants, and recycling paper. Other jobs change with the curriculum. For example, a postcard project, which the trips committee managed, only lasted a few months, while the math committee recorded the food brought in for the food pantry at the beginning of each month. Jobs that aren't necessary or current are taken off the list and new jobs are added. (Other examples of committee jobs are shown in Figure 1.)

As the year goes on, the children are able to take more responsibility for managing their committee meetings. This allows me to assume a less active role. By the third committee change in December, the children are usually able to reorganize and make the necessary committee changes without me.

Moderator's Duties

The job of class moderator rotates daily, alphabetically by first name. The moderator performs many of the jobs traditionally assigned to any "leader of the day": taking attendance to the office, leading the Pledge of Allegiance, getting things for the teacher, and so on. But in my class, the moderator, who sits in a special chair during our group meetings, also has specific leadership responsibilities. For example, he or she records the attendance and lunch count, feeds any animals we have in the room, checks the room after cleanup, calls children to line up before leading them to special classrooms, leads daily sharing, and calls on children to speak during a class meeting.

Class Meeting

Class meeting is a special time when we talk specifically about ways to strengthen our classroom community. We sit on chairs in a circle in order to distinguish class meetings from other times when we gather as a group.

I sit by the easel so that I can record the important points that come up, and write any rules we establish. Someone volunteers to take care of the minutes by copying what I've written and adding his or her own notes as well. The moderator helps run the class meeting by calling on children to speak and asking the group questions.

During class meeting, we discuss positive ways of working and playing together. We also concentrate on specific school-related problems that we need to solve so that our classroom will be a positive living and learning environment for everybody.

I write many of our decisions and rules on chart paper and put them up in the room so we can review them throughout the year and refer to them when a problem arises. The minutes are posted in the room.

"Talking the Problem"

I find that addressing problems formally in a class meeting helps us all to focus on the issue, take ownership of the problem, and be part of the solution. The procedure is just as important for me as for the children because it enables me to listen to their ideas and solutions.

One of the procedures we use to discuss specific school-related issues is called "talking the problem," which consists of the seven steps listed below (these steps are posted on a chart and always visible in the classroom):

1. State the problem.
2. Decide what we want to have happen.
3. Suggest ways to get this to happen.
4. Pick one solution.
5. Try this solution for two days.
6. Decide whether the solution was a good one.
7. If it wasn't, talk about the problem again.

Usually, I introduce "talking the problem" in September to familiarize the children with the procedure. For example, at the beginning of one year I noticed that during group time children were sitting up on their legs, which prevented those behind them from seeing. I heard frequent whispered comments: "Sit down." "I can't see." Some children were also talking to their neighbors or poking them, so that it was hard to pay attention.

During class meeting, we "talked the problem," using the seven steps. I wrote the responses on a special form, which we referred to throughout the school year.

Other important issues we've discussed by "talking the problem" have been whether to allow cutting in line, how to include every-one who wants to play tag on the playground, keeping the coat area orderly, cleaning up after snack time, cleaning up the room at the end of the day, and selecting books (the concern that Michael noted and put in the suggestion box).

An Ongoing Process
Trusting children to be responsible for their own learning and behav-ior is at the heart of establishing democratic procedures of class gov-ernment in my classroom. It's an ongoing process that involves my commitment to allow time and opportunities for the children to do their committee work, for the moderator to lead the class, and for all of us to participate in the class meetings.

It has also involved my willingness to take the time to talk about problems when they arise, to review procedures from time to time, and to change or modify the rules we have established when they don't support a positive classroom climate. The results are well worth the effort.

As children and teacher take the responsibility to participate in class government, it naturally follows that they can also be responsible for their own learning.

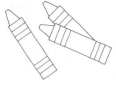

Supporting Reading Development in a First-Grade Classroom

I like to give my first graders many extended opportunities to practice reading as they develop as lifelong readers.

Moving from teaching kindergarten to first grade allowed me to observe firsthand what happens with emergent and beginning readers as they develop toward fluency, and to be involved in supporting their continued growth. I have extended many of the structures, strategies, and attitudes that formed the core of my kindergarten reading program. For example, my first-grade class still participates daily in shared reading, hears many stories, and writes every day. I continue to create an atmosphere in which the children feel comfortable with approximations, are willing to take risks, and perform as confident readers regardless of where they are on the reading continuum.

Quiet and Silent Reading

Every day after lunch recess, the children spend an hour reading (Fisher 1996). They begin by reading silently by themselves, move to quiet reading with a friend, and finish with shared reading with the whole class. Reading is defined broadly to include looking at pictures, making up stories, and/or reading the words at various levels of accuracy.

During silent reading, there is no talking or moving about the room, so the children have to select their books ahead of time. At the beginning of the year, we set a timer for five minutes, but within a month we extended the time to fifteen minutes. As the children become accustomed to the procedure, most of them are able to choose enough books for the allotted time.

Learning to select the appropriate number and the kinds of books that interest them is an important part of the process. They are free to choose from the selection of trade books, beginning readers, and magazines in the room, as well as read their library books and books from home. I suggest they pick one or two books that will help them "practice" their reading. Sometimes I give specific suggestions relative to one of their choices, such as to pick a book from the science area or to select a rhyming or predictable book.

At the end of fifteen minutes, the timer rings to signal the end of silent reading and the beginning of quiet reading. Although many children continue to read by themselves, they are now free to move about the room and read quietly with their friends. Some share the books they have been reading earlier, while others join together on the rug to read big books and charts or to sing songs. Reading time ends with shared reading followed by my reading a story to end the school day.

Independent, Teacher-Supported Reading
Envelope books
In this procedure (which we call "envelope" reading, because the children take books home in a manila envelope to read to their parents and then bring the books back to read with me) each child practices reading at her or his instructional level.

Early in the year, I explain the procedure to the class and meet with the children individually to help them select a few books to put in their envelopes to take home. Also in the envelope is a letter to parents describing the procedure and their role in it.

As a way of documenting their reading growth over time, the children keep a list of the "envelope" books they read during the year. I ask the parents to help them record the book title and date on an accompanying form and add a positive remark in the column for teacher and parent comments. Children are encouraged to bring the books back every three days, and place the envelope in a basket in the reading area of the room. Most of the children are consistent about bringing the books back, and I make certain that I read frequently with the few children who don't return their envelope books regularly.

During silent and quiet reading, and at other times in the day when I have a few free minutes, I take an envelope out of the basket and work with that child. We talk about the book, and the child reads it to me. I comment on her or his successes and help the child increase the use of appropriate strategies. For example, I might encourage the use of the beginning sound or letter of a word or acknowledge the use of picture cues to figure out a word. I might comment that, like other successful readers, I noticed that the child reread a sentence that didn't make sense.

I keep continuous records, noting the date, level of book read,

BOOKS I CAN READ	Name: _____		
DATE	TITLE	Practice Level*	PARENT/TEACHER COMMENT

* Practice level
E = Easy; R = Just Right; Ch = Challenge; H = Too Hard

FIGURE 1   *"Books I Can Read" chart*

strategies used or discussed, and ways to help the child in the future (Fisher 1995). We finish by discussing what book or books the child will take next, and sometimes we predict what a new selection will be about. I find that I read with each child about twice a week.

Book levels of difficulty
In order to facilitate appropriate selection of books and to assess progress, I have categorized the emergent and early reading books from the Story Box, Sunshine Books, Twig Books (Wright Group), and Literacy 2000 (Rigby) series into six levels, which form the core of books used in this independent, teacher-supported reading procedure. These levels are based on the levels the publishers have suggested as

well as on decisions I have made about their degree of difficulty as I have observed children reading them.

Level 1 is divided into seven parts, which correspond to the number of words on each of the eight pages in the book. For example, a 1–2 book such as *A Toy Box* (Literacy 2000) has two words on most of the pages: "A truck." "A spaceship." "A ball." "A doll." A 1-6 book, such as *My Friend* (Sunshine Books), has six or seven words on a page: "A tiger is not my friend." "A spider is not my friend." The books in Level 2 have between eight and fifteen words covering several lines on a page, and are eight or sixteen pages long. Level 3 has more text on sixteen or twenty-four pages. Levels 4 through 6 continue to increase in difficulty. The children are always allowed to choose other books in the room for "envelope" books as they grow into fluency.

I have organized these books in levels so that I can help each child at her or his instructional level. I believe that reading at instructional level is only one of the ways that children develop as readers, and should be one of the many reading opportunities in a classroom.

Reading throughout the day
Children are reading all the time in my classroom, and I want them to be aware of the varied and authentic reading that is going on, not just when they are reading a book, participating in shared reading, or hearing a story. Therefore, we keep an ongoing list of the different kinds of reading that happen in the classroom.

This list includes morning message, the clipboard list of things to do, the sign-in paper, estimation questions for math, letters from parents and visitors, shelf labels for math manipulatives, the children's own writing, big books, poems and songs on charts, writing demonstrations, and charts of all kinds displayed around the room. This list also helps to remind me that the children are practicing their reading throughout the day, and are becoming lifelong readers for a variety of purposes.

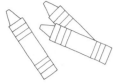

Trusting Individual Readers

Last September, after having taught kindergarten for eight years, I moved to first grade. I was looking forward to seeing firsthand what really happens with those emergent and early readers (and writers) as they develop toward fluency in first grade.

I took a third of my kindergartners with me. The others came from the class across the hall—a classroom much like my own.

All the children started first grade enjoying stories, joyfully participating during shared reading, feeling comfortable with approximations, willing to take risks, invested in their own writing, and free to "invent" spelling; all performed as confident readers regardless of where they were on the reading continuum.

As the year went on, I marveled at the progress the children were making in reading. By February most of them were early readers, and a few were becoming fluent. When I introduced a new text during shared reading, most of them could read right along as I pointed, and my voice could fade away on the first reading as they took over.

During quiet reading, most of them spent some of the time attending to the print and reading word for word. During collaborative reading, they helped each other read big books and trade books. As I watched and listened, I trusted that these children were learning. But what about those first graders who were still emergent readers, not independent readers?

Defining Terms

Reading stages and accompanying behaviors have been described in a variety of ways (Holdaway 1979; Cochrane et al. 1983; Wellington Department of Education 1985; Fisher 1991, 1995). The terms most generally used are *emergent* (making a start), *early* (becoming a reader), and *fluent* (going it alone) (Wellington Department of Education 1985).

In first grade, I focus on emergent readers who are operating at what I call print stage 1 and on my role in helping them move to print stage 2 and early reading. It is important to remember that these stages and accompanying descriptors are only general categories that help adults understand children's reading development. Every child's reading approach, progress, and experience are unique to him or her.

Emergent readers at print stage 1 are just beginning to watch the print when I point to the words as we read or sing during shared reading. With some accuracy, they can point word for word to short texts that are very familiar. They move back and forth from telling the story orally to reading slowly word for word, trying to match the words they know to the print. Familiarity of text is crucial to their success.

By the middle of first grade, most children are early readers and have moved into print stage 2. They demonstrate intense interest in watching the print during shared reading and can with accuracy point word for word to familiar texts. Also, they are taking control of the visual cueing system and are developing strategies to help with unfamiliar words. I find that children who move into print stage 2 with ease make the transition to becoming independent readers almost without my noticing. It seems that all at once they apply the semantic, syntactic, and graphophonemic cueing systems in concert with one another and are able to develop fluency with simple unfamiliar texts.

Moving Through Plateaus

But what about those few children who are still emergent readers, who are still at print stage 1? What can I do to help them become more independent and, at the same time, maintain their high self-confidence? The pressure from the adult world to "get" everyone reading independently by the end of first grade is enormous. When does the pressure affect the child, even in a supportive, noncompetitive classroom and school? What can I do to make certain that these pressures do not affect me or the child and address the individual and varied circumstances of these students?

I have to trust these children as learners, just as I have trusted the other children in the class, and I have to avoid the traditional teaching paradigm that compares children, focusing on what they cannot do rather than what they can do, and evaluating a single performance rather than their growth over time.

Guiding Growth

In the middle of the year, I evaluate the reading and writing progress of all the children in my class, including them in some aspect of this process. I listen to them read, examine their writing portfolios, and review the anecdotal notes I've taken throughout the year. I spend extra time assessing the children who are still emergent readers and look closely at what they can do, the progress they have made, and the literacy experiences that particularly engage them.

From there, I develop some guidelines for the direction I want to take with them for the rest of the year, working within their "zone of proximal development" (Vygotsky 1962).

When Maura reads, she loves to hold a book up as though she were reading to the class. She always wants to read with me and asks to lead the class in a "song" book such as *Mary Wore Her Red Dress* (Peek). She's beginning to use the graphophonic cues as she points and reads. During buddy reading with a third-grade partner, she reads book after book and seems very comfortable asking for help. One of my plans for Maura: provide more opportunities for her to buddy read.

Barron is just beginning to show interest in reading some of the small, predictable books in the classroom, and I notice that this has followed his recent involvement and progress in writing his own books. The writing he does is helping him learn how to read. One goal for Barron: give him more opportunities to share his writing.

John's reading and writing are coming along slowly, but when I look carefully at my records, I see progress. John is interested in science, and I notice that during quiet reading he spends most of his time looking at illustrations rather than attending to print. During writing time, he works on detailed drawings and often does not get to writing. It is sometimes difficult for him to tell me what he wants to say, although there is a wealth of ideas in his drawing. By himself, John gets distracted with the mechanics of writing, although when we work together, his spacing, invented spelling, and letter size are appropriate. However, when he is able to focus and write independently, he communicates fluidly using written language. A few of my plans for John: observe him more closely and figure out ways to capitalize on his interest in details; work with him individually, without taking ownership away; and give him ownership to choose when he is ready to write.

Hilary was in my kindergarten class, so I know that she has made a great deal of progress within the past year and a half. I also know that she needs repetition to learn something and that her mode of learning is social. She loves to read and sing favorite big books and songs with friends at the easel. She writes so she can sit in the author's chair and share in front of the class. She rushes through tasks that do not have a social context and is more engaged in writing when she works with a friend. My plan for Hilary: give her opportunities to learn collaboratively with her peers and help her see the value of doing some work alone.

Carol was also in my class last year, and I know that even though she has made progress, learning to read and write is not easy for her. She knows most of the letter names and some of the beginning consonant sounds, although auditory discrimination is difficult for her. However, she is highly motivated and confident of her progress. Either my assistant or I work with her individually every day. My plan for Carol: continue the daily individual help; ensure that her attitude remains positive; and discuss her progress with the school's Child Study Team and enlist their support in evaluating her learning profile and planning appropriate learning experiences. But, most important, I need to trust her as a learner and take my lead from her.

Jay enrolled in my kindergarten class last February, after being placed in a foster home in the community. His life has been inconsistent and disruptive, and he has not had the rich experiences of stories and conversations that have been woven into the lives of most of the other children in my class. Jay is very engaged during shared reading, while listening to stories and looking at books, and when drawing. He is an early emergent reader, although I notice that he is becoming quite accurate when pointing to familiar text. He is also confident using invented spelling. My plan for Jay: continue exposing him to the rich world of written and oral language, and trust him as a learner.

As I evaluate these emergent readers, I notice that they are all motivated, confident, and engaged in the learning environment in my classroom. Their progress indicates that they will soon become readers, if I trust them as learners, assist them in following their individual and natural interests, and provide them with supportive texts and meaningful, whole-literacy experiences.

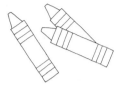

We *Do* Teach Phonics

As I talk with teachers around the country, I hear a recurring comment: *Many people think phonics isn't a part of holistic teaching, but I know that I'm continually addressing phonics in my class.*

Up until a few years ago, many kindergartners did "letter of the week" worksheets, and first and second graders completed phonics worksheets and workbook pages, which consisted primarily of isolated multiple-choice questions and fill-in-the-blank answers. Worksheets made up a large portion of the written work that children did at school, and many teachers and parents concluded that children learn to read primarily by knowing letters and sounding out words. The worksheets made it obvious to all that phonics was being taught.

Phonics is still being taught in holistic classrooms, but as part of the meaning-making process, not as isolated drill on worksheets and workbook pages. Children are learning to apply their knowledge of phonics strategically by reading meaningful texts and through their own writing. In these classrooms, teachers help children integrate the three language cueing systems—semantic, syntactic, and graphophonemic (see Figure 1)—as the children read (Goodman, Watson & Burke 1987).

Integrating the Reading Cueing System Through Song

Singing is important in my class because it draws us together as a community of learners and engages everyone, even the most reluctant learner. Songs are easy to learn and remember.

Unlike a storybook, which is best heard from beginning to end, a song doesn't have to be sung in its entirety in order to be understood and enjoyed. No matter how familiar we are with a song, we usually sing it through for enjoyment first before we respond to the text in detail.

I always call the children to the rug by singing. This clear signal engages those who have already gathered and gives others the opportunity to finish what they are doing before joining the group. Today I start singing a familiar and favorite song, "Habitat," by Peter and Mary Alice Amidon.

Using children's names

Then I hold up Merle Peek's book *Mary Wore Her Red Dress*. As we sing along, I point to the text, which has been written on a chart. I select Todd's name from a box of class names that I keep by my teaching easel, and I ask, "Whose name ends with the sound */d/?*" Todd raises his hand and we sing an innovation of the text: "Todd wore his green shirt." I follow the same procedure with a few more names, placing each one I've used in a separate pile, so that everyone will be chosen during the next two weeks.

Using children's names is one of the most meaningful ways to help children focus on letters and sounds because it draws them personally into the text. This time, we used ending letters and sounds in the children's names when we sang about what they were wearing. Other times, we've worked with beginning letters, medial consonants, vowels, and blends.

Introducing a new song

Next, I turn on the tape recorder and we all sing "Popcorn," a song by Rick Charette. Although I've written the words on a chart, I don't point to the text because this is the first time we've sung this song. There will be many opportunities to make the association with the written words as we become familiar with the song.

I hear a joyful buzz of conversation about popcorn. For now, the discussion centers on the children's personal experiences with popcorn as I ask them to share quietly with the person next to them. These informal, small-group moments of sharing, which last no more than a minute or two, include the children's personal stories of the times they had popcorn as well as their reactions to the stories in the song.

Discussions of a new text primarily address the semantic cueing system, although syntax and graphophonics continually come into play. With "Popcorn," we start from a reader-response perspective—talking about what the text reminds us of in our own lives and telling personal stories that relate to the text (Tompkins & McGee 1993; Fisher 1995). In subsequent singings, we'll discuss various particulars of the text.

Activities with favorite songs

Next, we sing "Baby Beluga," by Raffi, a favorite song that we know well from having sung it numerous times. I use the song to discuss various skills and strategies, focusing specifically on the graphophone-mic cueing system, but always within the context of meaning and syntax. I start by asking the children what they notice on the chart and we build our discussion from there.

For example, I say, "I notice that Baby and Beluga start with *b*, just like my name." I slowly run my pointer under the text and ask the children to say the sound /*b*/ whenever I come to the letter *b*. Then we sing the song one more time, listening for the /*b*/ as we go along.

Although we are focusing on a particular letter, the children are also becoming familiar with other letters as they compare and distinguish different features. For example, they have to distinguish between the *d*s and *b*s in the first line, "Baby Beluga in the deep blue sea."

"I notice that you drew a picture of water around the word *sea*," someone comments. Building on this, I write the words *sea* and *see* in two columns on the chart paper on my easel, and we discuss two spellings for the long /*e*/ sound in these words.

We find other words in the text and add words we know. Someone notices that *baby* and *me* have /*e*/ sounds, so we add two more columns. This exercise, which takes about five minutes, addresses phonics and spelling in a meaningful context.

Next, I point to the word *little* and we start generating a list of words we know that mean about the same as *little*, and then a list of words that mean the opposite. As someone says a word, I spell it out loud, comment about the letters and sounds, and write the word on a sticky note. We place the word on the song and sing the line, checking to confirm that the new word makes sense and sounds right.

Then we sing another favorite song, "Gravity," which repeats the phrase, "G-r-a-v-i-t-y, gravity's the thing," as the song discusses how gravity affects different nursery-rhyme characters.

From there, we generate a list of other things that are important to us; for example, *playing*, *running*, and *friendship*. We sing these words in place of *gravity* when we sing the song again. Later in the day, the children will select one of the words and make their own page for a class book.

What's Happening Here

Throughout this singing part of the shared literacy session, all three language cueing systems have repeatedly come into play. I have continually asked the children to focus on semantics (Does it make sense?) and syntax (Does it sound right?). These two cueing systems are con-

Cueing System	Focus	Question
Semantic	Meaning	Does it make sense?
Syntactic	Sound of the language	Does it sound right?
Graphophonemic	Letters and sounds	Do the letters and sounds match what we know about the word? Does the word look right?

FIGURE 1 *Language cueing systems*

nected because if something doesn't sound right, it usually doesn't make sense. We've also addressed the graphophonic cueing system: Does the word look right? Do the letters and sounds predict and/or confirm the word in the text?

I believe that if we, as teachers, want children to apply their letter and sound knowledge, we must demonstrate how to do this strategically as we read. Naming letters and saying sounds in an isolated oral drill or practicing them on a worksheet is not part of the reading process. Letters and sounds are difficult to learn in isolation because there's no basis for comparing and contrasting them, or for learning to predict where they occur in the printed text.

In order to be meaning makers, children must participate in authentic demonstrations of the integration of the three cueing systems through meaningful experiences with a variety of favorite, familiar texts.

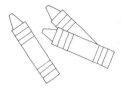

Writing Workshop in a First-Grade Classroom

Writing workshop is an essential part of the curriculum in my first-grade classroom; almost every morning the children do some self-selected writing.

On a typical day, you might observe two children talking together about a book they're planning to write, several children involved in work they had started the day before, others beginning a piece they will finish that day, a few starting a story they will work on for a longer period of time.

You'd probably also see a group of children sitting in a circle discussing their work, and someone hanging a finished piece on the sharing bulletin board or putting it in the basket to share with the class later. Most likely I'd be having a writing conference with a student. Finally, at the end of writing time, we might all sit in a circle on the floor with our current work in front of us, sharing some descriptive words that we've included in our pieces.

The following elements help me create a dynamic and meaningful writing workshop for my first graders: a positive attitude of trust and commitment; an understanding of the process of writing; an orderly arrangement of materials; a predictable daily routine; a clearly defined role for me as the teacher; and my ongoing professional reading.

Trust and Commitment

Since I believe that writing is essential for literacy development, I am committed to providing time for writing every day.

The children trust that they'll have daily opportunities to pursue their own topics, work by themselves or with friends, and begin a new piece or work on a story or book over time. I trust that when given these choices, they'll become engaged in meaningful, rigorous, and lasting learning.

These conditions provide me with opportunities to support the children in their growth as writers through minilessons, individual conferences, publishing opportunities, and whole-class sharing.

The Process of Writing

Building on the work of Lucy Calkins (1994), Don Graves (1994), and Donald Murray (1989), over the years I've created my own descriptions of the different procedures of writing—rehearsal, drafting, revising, and editing—to guide my teaching. I've also added a fifth procedure: sharing.

- Rehearsal—different ways that children plan what to write. This includes thinking, talking, and reading. It often occurs while the children are writing, not just before they begin.
- Drafting—the actual writing of the piece. This is often interspersed with thinking and talking.
- Revising—going over what is written. This happens continually as children write, not just during that last time before the work is edited or declared finished.
- Editing—working with an editor (teacher, parent, or another student) to prepare the piece for publication. This includes attending to meaning and working on standardizing writing conventions and spelling. The extent of editing varies. It can entail helping the child make a few appropriate changes directly on the original or preparing the piece to be published in conventional form, either printed on the computer or copied by the student.
- Sharing—all the different ways that children share their work. This includes producing a computer-printed piece, sharing in the author's chair, hanging the piece on the sharing board, taking it home, adding it to their portfolio, or simply showing it to a friend.

Organization of Materials

A systematic organization of supplies and writing folders is essential for writing workshop. In my classroom, general writing supplies are easily available and are organized and maintained by the children.

Pencils, crayons, erasers, rulers, staplers, date stamps, and a variety of sizes of paper, both lined and unlined, are located in the writing area. In the reading area, there are dictionaries and lists of frequently used and descriptive words that hang on the area's bulletin board. Lists of social studies, science, and math words, which are generated by the class throughout the year, are posted in the corresponding areas.

There are five work tables in my classroom, and five children are assigned to each table for eight weeks. Each table has a plastic file box with a hanging file for each child. In the hanging file are pocket folders in which the children keep their ongoing writing, personal dictionaries, lists of topic suggestions, and other papers. Completed work is filed in a monthly file; at the end of each month, children choose a few pieces for their yearly portfolio.

Predictable Daily Routine

When the children arrive in the morning, one of their jobs is to get ready for writing. They put their folders at their chosen places and get any paper and supplies they'll need. Some choose to work at their assigned tables, while others settle in at other places around the room.

Many of the children have already begun writing even before we formally start the day as a group on the rug. After this shared literacy time, which often concludes with a writing minilesson, the children return to their chosen places and begin.

Writing time winds down very naturally. When children are finished, they put away their work and move to the rug to read while waiting for sharing time.

Being finished means a variety of things. It could mean that a piece is completely done, in which case the children put it in the sharing basket (which means they would like to sit in the author's chair and share it with the class) or hang it on the sharing board or file it in their monthly file. It could also mean that they are finished working on the piece for the day and will continue with it tomorrow. In this case, they file it in their pocket folder at their table.

WRITING CONFERENCE RECORDING FORM Name: _____						
DATE	GENRE	MEANING CONTENT	CONVENTIONS	TEACHING OPPORTUNITIES	NEXT STEPS

FIGURE 1 *Recording form*

My role as a writing teacher is most apparent during shared literacy, when I work with the entire class, and during writing workshop, when I confer with individual children.

Through the day, I read aloud four or five books to the class. This extensive reading, along with accompanying discussions, supports the children as writers. They hear different genres and models of written language and discuss the various ways that authors express themselves.

I also conduct minilessons focusing on specific areas of writing. Carol Avery, in *And with a Light Touch* (1993), offers the following categories of minilesson: *procedures* (e.g., using a writing folder); *strategies writers like* (e.g., using books to inspire topics); *qualities of good writing* (e.g., adding information for the sake of clarity); and *skills* (e.g., using capital letters to start sentences).

After a minilesson, writing workshop begins. I usually sit at one of the tables and start my own writing. I then start working with individual children. Sometimes I move from table to table and hold conferences. The children might tell me what they're working on; I might notice something about their piece or help them with a word they've tried to spell on their "have a go" paper.

Periodically, I guide a more in-depth conference with each child and fill in a writing conference form. We discuss the meaning of the piece: what it's about, where the student got the idea, and where he or she thinks the piece is headed. We also discuss some of the writing conventions the child has been working on: what he or she has done successfully, what he or she is ready to focus on next. We talk about

Name: MICHAEL	Have-a-go		Date: JAN 3
PIIEEISEISSE	PIOIEE	police	POLICE
RUIUD	BUUD	build	PUILD
hAIMET	hAMMET	helmet	hALMET
AhoAMIPS	ANAMIS	animals	ANiMAIS

FIGURE 2 *Have a go*

spelling strategies for a few important words in the piece. Finally, we discuss the child's future writing plans.

Professional Reading

I continue to refine and develop my writing workshop as I observe children writing; and as I read professionally and incorporate new ideas into my teaching. Currently I've been reading the following books:

A Fresh Look at Writing (Heinemann, 1994): Don Graves describes ways to confer with students to help them focus on topic choice and clarify what they need to do next in their writing.

The Art of Teaching Writing (new edition, Heinemann, 1994): Lucy Calkins expands on the first edition and deepens our understanding of the reading/writing connection.

And with a Light Touch: Learning About Reading, Writing, and Teaching with First Graders (Heinemann, 1993): Writing from her experience as a first-grade teacher, Carol Avery describes the way she integrates reading and writing workshop and encourages her children to read like writers and write like readers.

Questions and Answers About Spelling

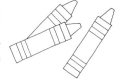

Is Spelling Important?

Yes, spelling is important as one of the language systems that support communication. I believe that it is best learned through use in authentic literacy situations. Spelling is first addressed globally and then becomes more specific, a process that takes many years of reading and writing and is certainly not to be accomplished in the first few years of school.

What Do You Keep in Mind as You Work with Spelling with Young Children?

When I think of spelling with young children, I focus on the learner. Spelling involves thinking; it is not a random guessing game or an isolated memorization activity but is based on what the child knows. Spelling involves taking risks: a word often isn't spelled correctly the first time. Spelling involves an attitude: we need authentic reasons in order to work toward accuracy. Spelling involves our social, emotional, intellectual, and cultural context.

How Is Spelling Addressed in Your First Grade?

I believe that children learn spelling in much the same way they learn to talk and read. Therefore, the conditions of natural learning (Cambourne 1988) provide a theoretical framework for spelling in my class. The children are *immersed* in a print-rich environment in my classroom, and are involved in *demonstrations* of spelling-related strategies such as phonetics, invented spelling, phonics rules, word families, rhyming words, root words, and memorization, all within the context of a whole text. Through active participation during shared reading, children are *engaged* in a playful dialogue about spelling. Because their reading and writing is meaningful to them, they take the *responsibility* to attend to spelling. I have the *expectation* that their spelling will become more conventional over time. I know that this will happen as children feel free to *approximate* and are given *feedback* and opportunities to *use* what they are learning about spelling in authentic situations.

How Do You Help the Children Focus on Spelling Throughout the Year?

At the beginning of the year I encourage invented spelling as the most important spelling strategy because I want the children to feel confident in their ability to get their ideas down on paper. Throughout the year I support spelling development in different ways. During shared reading the children are exposed to conventional spelling through extensive reading of enlarged text and intensive discussion of individual words. During writing they focus individually at their own developmental level on spelling patterns, rules, and conventions. They continually internalize correct spelling as they observe, practice, and discuss spelling.

What Are Your Views on Invented Spelling?

If we view spelling as a developmental process, invented spelling becomes the starting point for young children to work toward conventional spelling. We can observe this development through the children's invented spelling, which is the spelling they create from their knowledge about spelling, and from their ever-increasing use of conventional patterns and spellings. Other terms used for invented spelling are *functional spelling* or *temporary spelling*; in my class the terms *ear spelling* and *eye spelling* have been helpful to the children.

Children as Authorities on Their Own Writing

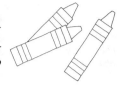

In my first-grade class we just call it writing, although it consists of both writing and drawing. It happens every day after a group time of singing, hearing a story, personal sharing, a shared writing experience or minilesson, and "anything else" we need to discuss as the day begins. This past June, "anything else" involved having the children help me prepare to interview them about their writing during the year.

I started by sharing with them some articles I had published and telling them I wanted to write an article about what they thought about writing. I explained that writing the article would help me understand what they did and what was important to them so I could be a better teacher next year, and that their ideas would also help other teachers who read the article.

Next, I showed them the notes I had written that morning to get me started—to remind me of what I wanted to say to them. We talked briefly about the four areas of the writing process I would be asking about in the interviews: how they got their ideas for writing (rehearsal); what they did as they began (drafting); what they did to check over their writing (revision); and how they shared their work (publishing). I explained that I would also be asking their opinions about "silent" and "quiet" writing.

In my class, we write for about forty minutes every morning. In the middle of this period, a timer is set for about ten minutes of silent or quiet writing. The children have choices of paper, writing utensils, and topic. They can write books or produce a single piece, and can work alone or collaborate. During writing time, I confer with individuals or groups of writers, and spend time on my own writing. At the end of writing on most days, one or two children sit in the author's chair to share their work with the class. A few times a year I demonstrate the procedure of writing a book to be published on the computer, and everyone participates in the assignment, which takes about a week.

As I observed my first graders deeply involved in writing this year, I noticed that they were in control of their own writing process. From the start they had set their own rules. Rather than consciously work separately and sequentially on each of the four "steps" of the writing process, they were immersed in their own "stuff" as a single process, interchangeably rehearsing, drafting, revising, and publishing as they went along. I had provided the materials, time, and atmosphere for their idiosyncratic process to emerge.

Now I wanted to ask them about it. How did they plan what they were going to write, or did they plan? How did they go about their actual writing? Did they revise their work, and, if so, what did they do? How did they share their work? What did they like or dislike about quiet and silent writing? They were writers now, but did they want to be writers when they grew up? These six questions were the basis of the individual interviews I conducted with the twenty-two first graders in my class.

How Do You Get Your Ideas for Writing?

The children indicated a variety of sources for topics: from their own experience, by drawing, by talking, and by thinking. However, it was clear that the most powerful source came from books—trade books and books written by themselves and classmates.

"I look at books."

"I get ideas from books other kids made."

"From books I have made."

"I look at the shapes on the covers of books."

What had I done throughout the year to help the children make the connection between the published work of others and their own writing? We had read many books and talked about the choices authors and illustrators make. For example, in discussing a specific word in a book, I often mentioned that although the author decided to use one word, if they were the author, they might choose a different one. We read like writers, and the children began to write like readers.

Jenna was the only child who talked at length about the importance of talk during writing time as a way of getting ideas: "I get ideas from other people. We talk at our table."

Why didn't more of the children mention talk as a source for topics? There is a lot of talk going on in my classroom while we write. Children are continually talking about what they are doing, either when working on their own piece or when collaborating. Is it true that there isn't much talk about topic selection, or are the children unaware that they are selecting through talk? Is most of the talk about work in

process, once the topic is selected? These are questions I want to con-
sider next year as I observe children more specifically as they write.

63

*Children as
Authorities on
Their Own
Writing*

How Do You Start Writing and What Do You Do When You Write?

Although almost every child mentioned drawing as part of his or her
response, there were many interpretations of my question, and each
child had a special entry point that signaled the start of writing.

For some, it began with the physical setup. A.J. said, "I get my
stuff, get in the chair, and think about how it looks." Ryan reported,
"I take a piece of paper and write."

Several mentioned they started by writing specific words. Amy
writes *Once upon a time* . . . Chelsea said, "I think about what I'm going to do. Usually I use the words *I am* . . ." Julianna thinks of names
and pictures and then writes *This is a* . . . James starts by "trying to
spell it."

Several children used the word *think* to describe what they did.
Stevie said, "I draw first . . . write a little, and think before and during
writing." Victor explained, "I erase what I'm thinking [in my mind],
and put it on my paper." Tony stated, "I think what's the sentence so
it makes sense."

What had I done as a teacher to demonstrate how one starts
writing? When the children saw me write, either during group time or
when I wrote by myself, I picked up the pencil and began. Every day
at the end of group time, I just said, "Start writing," and that comment signaled it was time to go to their self-selected writing place and
begin. Each morning when the children came in, they got their writing ready by putting their writing folder and materials at their writing
place. To my recollection, no formal conversation about the topic of
how one begins writing ever took place.

Next year I plan to discuss what starting writing can mean, although I still expect that I will get a variety of responses. After all, if
someone asked me what I did to start writing, I would probably say
that I turn on my computer. When pressed further about getting the
written message down, I would say that I type the words that I'm
thinking and then I see what I have written. Very likely that descrip-
tion may not be what I do at all. Describing writing is difficult, but I
believe that all writers, children and adults alike, can profit from trying
to do so. I also plan to spend more time demonstrating what I do
when I write, by talking through my thinking as I compose in front of
the class and then encouraging the children to participate in the writing (Graves 1991).

Do You Check Over Your Work After You Have Written?

I was surprised at the detailed responses I received to this question, their specificity indicating that all the children were revising their work.

"I make lots of corrections."

"I read it over and see if things are right. I ask someone and use my ear spelling."

"I read and change for an idea or for a word."

"Sometimes I write so fast that I forget how to spell a word. I can mess up."

"I reread so I know what to do next."

"I want to be sure I put everything I want to put. I don't want to have any bad writing."

During the year, the children had participated in several kinds of writing situations in which revising had been demonstrated: when I wrote in front of the entire class, as we edited a student's work on the overhead projector, and during individual conferences. Often, as a general announcement, I would remind the children to read over their work and make any changes when they finished.

During group time, as we wrote group letters, lists, and stories, we reread our work, made corrections, crossed out, and added others. Often as I wrote, children would correct my mistakes before we had a chance to reread together. We talked about mistakes as a way of learning. As part of individual writing conferences with me, children made changes, additions, and corrections, and I demonstrated editing techniques such as crossing out and writing above the word, making two lines to indicate the separation of words, and using the carat to show the insertion of a word.

Occasionally, with the child's permission, I would put a piece of writing on the overhead projector for the class to discuss. After the author read the piece, he or she would call on the audience (teacher included) to ask questions and to tell something positive they noticed about the writing. Typical responses were *I notice that you can spell the word cake . . . that you left spaces between the words . . . that you used lots of lowercase letters . . . that you put a period at the end.* Next, the author would add his or her "noticings" and then would tell anything he or she wanted to change. I would mark the changes on the overhead. At the end, we would sit in a circle and discuss what we learned and how we felt about the experience.

I feel satisfied with many of the ways that I helped children with revision. However, most of the writing revisions focused on mechanics and spelling; content revisions were almost exclusively limited to illustrations. I have a lot of questions to explore about content revision next year. Is there a time in a child's writing development when I am most likely to observe it? Where does revision of illustration fit in? What other factors are part of revision? If I demonstrate more content revision, will I notice it in the children's work?

How Do You Share Your Work?

For the majority of children, sharing their work meant sitting in the author's chair (Hansen & Graves 1983), reading their piece, and calling on classmates for "noticings" and questions. Every child liked doing this but stated that there weren't enough opportunities. Victor summed up the feelings this way: "I like the author's chair. I learn when I am in it, and I learn how it feels to be up there. When I listen, I listen to how people write. It gives me ideas. I take pieces of theirs and put them into mine."

Informal ways of sharing included reading to friends, showing people, and talking at their tables. Although most of the children wished there were more opportunities to sit in the author's chair, and liked sharing informally, many indicated that sharing wasn't particularly important to them, they just liked to write.

The children usually wrote single pieces or handwritten books. Single pieces, which included a picture and writing, were usually finished in a day. Handwritten books, either stapled together by me or constructed by the children, took anywhere from a day to several weeks to complete. There was a lot of variety within these formats, and throughout the year the children shifted back and forth between writing single pieces and handwritten books, and between working independently and collaboratively.

Each child also had two books published on the computer. I initiated the "assignment" and they went through a formal process of separate steps of prewriting, drafting, revising, and publishing. Although the finished computer product seemed acceptable to the children, I did not notice the investment and enthusiasm that was always evident when they were engaged in the free-choice writing of single pieces and handwritten books.

There is a lot of discussion among teachers and administrators about the value of computer-published books. The responses of my students indicated that the procedure of drafting, editing with an adult, publishing on the computer (usually with an adult inputting and making further editorial changes without the children being present), and finally adding illustrations to the final product was not as meaningful to first graders. The important writing for my children seemed to be the creative process of drawing and strategically placing words on the page. Their books burst forth spontaneously as pictures and writing were added interchangeably. When finished and put in the class library, the dynamic, sometimes ripped, often crayon-smudged child-stapled books that these self-proclaimed first-grade authors produced on their own were "read" more frequently than the computer-published ones. Graves warns of

> orthodoxies in our teaching that prevent us from being sensitive to writers. Some of these orthodoxies, or maxims for teaching, are necessary for temporary sanity as coping mechanisms for our teaching situations, or our personal need to overuse something in order to understand it. Often, something like publishing meets our own needs as teachers at the expense of what is best for the children. Publishing is visible evidence that "I am a productive teacher." Through engagement during writing time and pride in their work, the children tell me, "We are productive writers." That is evidence enough for me to know that "I am a productive teacher." (1984, p.192)

Next year, I want to study in more depth the relationship between children's engagement and the quality of the final products of both handwritten and computer published books. I plan to experiment with alternative approaches to encourage final products and different ways to share. Without a doubt, I will give more opportunities for everyone to sit in the author's chair.

Did You Like Silent and Quiet Writing?
All the children said they liked having ten minutes of silent or quiet writing as part of writing time every day. Silent meant *No talking*, and quiet meant *You can talk if you really have to*. The children created these definitions, and before writing began they decided which kind of time it would be for the day.

Six of the children preferred silent writing, five favored quiet, and half of the class liked both. They liked silent writing "because I can concentrate," and quiet writing "so we can talk a little" and "talk with people if you are doing a book together." Tony, who spent four months writing a book with Ian, said that he liked quiet writing "so you can show something that is really neat."

I was not surprised that everyone liked quiet and silent writing, since they had responded to it so positively throughout the year. I will continue the practice next year, although it could be argued that it goes against an orthodoxy that suggests that children must be allowed to talk as they write. I certainly value the importance of talk during writing, and there is plenty of time for that in my classroom, especially during writing. But I also value the intense and consistent commitment to writing and the quality of the product that this silent and quiet time produced. Again, Graves tells us,

> There are ways to protect against the establishment of orthodoxies. The first requires us to let children teach us about what they know. As long as we work hard to place the initiative in the child's corner, observe what the child is doing and telling us, and adjust our teaching to fit child growth, then orthodoxies shift. (1984, p.193).

From watching what the children did during daily writing and listening to what they told me during the interviews, I know that silent and quiet writing supported them in their literacy growth.

Do You Think You Will Be a Writer When You Grow Up?
I received a variety of answers to this question, and all but three children said yes, although many added something else, such as football player, policeman, taxi driver, and teacher. Chelsea is going to be a writer and a reader. Julianna is going "to write stories about things that happen in my life." Four children said they were going to be illustrators of children's books. These student responses directly mirrored the modeling and demonstrations that had gone on in the class in three ways.

First, the interviews indicated that the children primarily viewed writing as a separate occupation. This perception corresponded to the separate writing time that went on in my class. Also, although we read books and talked about authors, we didn't make many connections between writers and the content of what they had written. For example, we wrote during science, but we didn't talk at length about scientists as writers.

Second, several children said they wanted to be a teacher and a writer. Although first graders often say they want to be teachers, these children had a teacher who is also a writer. Eight had been in my kindergarten class and were either mentioned or pictured in my book *Joyful Learning: A Whole Language Kindergarten.* Many of them own my book, which I have signed for them, and there are copies in the classroom and school library. I show them articles I have written, and sometimes I work on articles when we are writing in the classroom. In eliciting their help for these articles, I show them that teachers can be writers. The children have had authentic demonstrations and modeling from a teacher/writer.

Third, the children who wanted to be illustrators very likely identified with the frequent discussions we had about the illustrators of and illustrations in the books we read. My assistant, Liz Schreiner, who is a professional artist, shared her work with the class. She discussed and demonstrated various illustrators' techniques and styles, and planned art experiences in which the children practiced using them.

Next year, I want to reflect on the benefits and shortcomings of keeping writing time separate and make a more concerted effort to help the children see themselves as scientists, historians, and mathematicians who also write and draw. I want to invite people of different occupations to come in and share ways that writing affects their work. I want to expand the children's perspective of who writers are and what they do.

These interviews demonstrated that the children were authorities on their own writing. In varying degrees, they were aware of where they got their ideas, what they did to start writing, the value of checking their work, and the power of sharing. They understood clearly that a quiet or silent time for writing helped them as writers. They saw themselves as writers now, and in the future.

Workshop Time:
Generating Curriculum

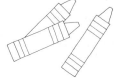

To engage children in authentic learning within the framework of a positive classroom community, I set up structures in my classroom workshops to support children in generating their own curriculum from topic work.

Generative Curriculum

Generative curriculum is a term that Pat Cordeiro and I use to describe the dynamic learning that takes place when children pursue their own individual and collective interests. One of my goals is to help children generate their own topics of interest and ways of learning as they engage in meaningful inquiry (Cordeiro 1995; Fisher 1995).

It's easier to say this than to do it; it takes a lot of organizing, planning, and demonstrating on my part. In a generative curriculum, the children take control of reading, writing, and other forms of expression while pursuing their own topics, and one interest generates another.

In my classroom, generative curriculum is most evident during workshop, which is scheduled two or three times a week for about an hour. During this interactive time, the children explore books and create projects as they pursue their own topics of inquiry or contribute to projects that have developed from small-group or whole-class topics. Workshop allows for multiple expression through the arts: painting, 3-D constructions, murals, drama, puppetry, block building, and science experiments. Workshop *isn't* a free-wheeling time when children wander around and do whatever they want.

Demonstrations of Possibilities

One way I guide children in generating curriculum is through demonstrations of possibilities that reflect Don Holdaway's (1979) natural learning classroom model in action: the different ways that learners gather information (demonstration and participation), create projects and artifacts (practice/role-play) and share (performance) what they have learned as they actively pursue curriculum interests. Demonstrations of possibilities encompass how children represent, portray, depict, illustrate, express, practice, explain, create, invent, communicate, describe, display, exhibit, experiment, produce, and express learning.

At the beginning of the year, I give many demonstrations of possibilities and sometimes require that the children try them. I add demonstrations throughout the year, building on the children's interests and literacy development. Very soon, they come up with their own demonstrations; one demonstration generates possibilities for another. The main categories of these demonstrations, which express themselves in the children's final products, include writing, extensions and innovations, the visual arts, 3-D building, note taking, interviews, surveys, and mini–field trips.

Writing

Children write every day in my classroom and they participate in writing demonstrations. They write one-page narratives, storybooks, and information books. During workshop, they often continue, adapt, and extend their personal writing, as well as create new writing projects to support their topics of inquiry.

Extensions and innovations

Extensions and innovations encourage children to make connections between a familiar book, poem, or song and current areas of interest and inquiry. They keep the same syntax and general format of the original. One child or a group of children can contribute a page to a new class text, or an individual or small group can make its own text.

Extensions retain the original text and either give more information or tell what might happen next. My class extended Michael Grater's six-book series *On Sunday the Giant . . .* , which ended with *On Friday the Giant . . .* , by writing *On Saturday the Giant . . .*

On the other hand, innovations substitute new text for the original text. David Drew's *Somewhere in the Universe* was the model for a book the children made as they studied the universe, a topic that was generated from the interests of a few children during workshop. After everyone had become familiar with the book through repeated readings, each child made his or her own book with himself or herself as the main character. On a street map of our town, each marked where his or her house was located, and then they all drew themselves on maps of Massachusetts, the United States, the earth, and the solar system.

Visual arts

Children also express themselves through the visual arts. Throughout the year, they witness demonstrations and gain experience using art materials such as crayons, paint, clay, paper, wood, and recycled materials to draw pictures, create murals, and make 3-D artifacts. One year, a group of children created a collage mural of animal life above and below ground.

3-D building

Many topics of inquiry are successfully explored and expressed through 3-D building. Materials include blocks (unit blocks, geoblocks, and pattern blocks), other math manipulatives (rods, Unifix cubes), recycled construction materials, and paper (origami, pop-up books). As part of the school-prescribed curriculum about Native Americans of the southwest, several teams of children used unit blocks to create scenes from Gerald McDermott's *Arrow to the Sun*.

Note taking

I introduce note taking early in the year and continue to demonstrate possibilities as the year goes on. I encourage the children to take notes while I read, and I offer opportunities for note taking from visual observations (a nature walk around the school yard) as well as from texts. Notes can be in the form of pictures and/or words, depending on the child's literacy development and learning style, as well as the subject matter.

Interviews

Interviewing possibilities abound in a generative curriculum. Early in the year, the children see this as a normal way to gather information, since I interview them about their reading, writing, math, and learning interests.

I demonstrate how to plan and conduct an interview, and during group time I choose someone to interview. The children help me draft appropriate questions and I conduct the interview. Next, the children interview each other. They gain experience as they interview school personnel, family members, and experts in various fields.

Surveys

Surveys are a simple form of interviewing. On the first day of school, I introduce the children to a class list in box form and teach them to check off their name when they complete a task. I start a survey, asking them to write their favorite number in the box with their name and we graph the results. This beginning generates different surveys and graphs invented by the children, and they continue to be produced throughout the year. The children survey their classmates about their favorite color, food, sport, number, etc.

Mini–field trips

Mini–field trips are excursions taken on school property. Sometimes we go as an entire class. Other times, teams of two or three set out to obtain information. (These trips are always inside.) Almost always, the children use clipboards so they can take notes. Possibilities for mini–field trips include a five-senses walk, texture rubbings, and a search with a magnet to record what things throughout the school are magnetic.

Sharing

Sharing (performance) is an essential part of a generative curriculum. It completes the cycle of the natural learning model, and it often starts a new learning cycle. As the children share what they've learned, they become the demonstrators or teachers. Throughout the day in my class, there are opportunities for incidental, informal, and formal kinds of sharing.

During workshop, there's a lot of incidental sharing as children work and talk with each other. For example, a group working on a papier mâché mobile of the planets examined books together as they decided what size balloon to use for each planet. They talked as they worked and shared what they were doing.

Informal sharing takes place at the end of workshop and it gives many children an opportunity to share. "Circle" share is when we all bring our work to the rug and briefly explain what we've been doing and how it's going. For "quick share," I hold up the children's work and make a few comments. In "around the room" share, everyone moves from one area to another to see and hear what individuals or groups have done.

Formal sharing is more elaborate and involves planning. A simple example is when a child or a group of children present their work in front of the class and take comments from the audience. More ceremonial sharing includes creating and participating in plays, festivals, fairs, video presentations, and the different components of visitors' days.

Authentic Interests

I have described some of the demonstrations of possibilities that I encourage during workshop to support children in generating curriculum around their own interests. As the year progresses, these structures are integrated with reading, writing, math, social studies, and science. Often, the daily schedule looks like a long workshop as the children make connections within and between disciplines.

For instance, I read Chris Van Allsburg's *The Two Bad Ants* to the class and someone found a science book about ants. Someone else wrote a home/adventure/home book with an ant as the main character. Another topic was generated when someone drew a maze, and we were all drawn into the stories of Daedalus, Icarus, and Theseus. A mural developed and the children used rules and learned about parallel lines as they drew their own mazes.

The generative curriculum is endless, because children are continually engaged in pursing their own authentic interests.

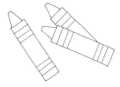

Writing Information Books in First Grade

After April vacation, with nine weeks of school remaining, I wanted to strengthen and refine the learning and classroom community that had developed over the year by combining writing and workshop with committee work. We started by forming new committees around a common topic of interest. Along with performing the usual committee jobs, every child wrote a book using the information shared by committee members.

Forming the Committees

Deciding the committee topics was an essential part of the process. We looked at a variety of science books and generated a list of possible topics, which we narrowed down to five: birds, nests, and eggs; bones and the human body; insects and bugs; animals and the five senses; and seeds and plants. The children wrote down their first three choices on a piece of paper and I formed the committees that afternoon after school.

When the children came in the next morning, they found a list of the new committees on the bulletin board. There was a lot of talk and activity as they rearranged the room and as committees negotiated for places to work. The seeds and plants committee moved to a table near the window, and the insect committee claimed the rolling bulletin board. Members gathered books and artifacts relating to their topic and arranged them on shelves and in boxes in their area. Many children got paper and started writing about their topic.

Writing the Book

The children worked on their information books for about a week during writing/workshop. We decided that the books should have at least five pages, but many wrote more. Danielle's book, *Things About Animals: Information Book*, had eight pages, and Michael wrote a series of six books about plants and seeds.

Although I introduced the basic procedure and format for the information books, the children generated their own ideas and became demonstrators along with me as they talked at their tables and shared in the large group. Consequently, each book represented the voice and style of its author. Elizabeth's book, for example, had a story quality. She included her feelings about plants. Andrew's book told about different insects, and Julie put a lot of diagrams in her book entitled *How Ears Work*.

Day 1

We started by looking at the big book *The Survival of Fish* (Biddulph & Biddulph) during shared literacy. We surveyed the book, examining its table of contents and index, text, section headings, photographs, drawings, and diagrams. On the easel, I wrote some guidelines of what the first information page should include: a picture, a sentence with some information, a diagram, and a title telling what the page is about. This got everyone started, but still offered flexibility and gave me a way to help the children who needed direction.

At the end of the work time, the children sat in a circle on the rug with their papers and an information book they had used. In turn, they shared what they had done and how things had gone for them. Alex read what he had written, Chris had put markers at the pages he wanted to show, and Sarah explained that she spent most of the time looking at books about her topic.

Day 2

The next morning, the children started working immediately when they came in. They were so engaged in continuing with their books that I delayed starting group. When we gathered for shared literacy, I held up a trade book from each topic group and gave a brief book talk about each.

I drew attention to the table of contents and index and demonstrated how the headings throughout the books matched those in the contents list. I wanted the children to think about the difference between the title for their book and the individual title for each page. I read a little piece from each book and we talked about how it related to the title the author had selected for that particular section. During workshop, I talked with the children about the title of the page they were working on and checked to be sure everyone had included it.

Day 3

The focus for shared literacy on this day was to help the children write the text in their own words. They were fascinated to hear about plagiarism laws, and we talked about stories we knew that had been retold by an author. I also showed them how to use quotation marks when using someone's exact words. After reading a section on fish survival, a child told in her own words what she had learned and I wrote it on the easel paper. During workshop, the children continued working on their books.

Day 4

By the fourth day, many children had written more than four pages and were indicating that they were almost finished. In preparation for writing the table of contents and index, we talked again about possible book titles, and they checked to see that each page had a different heading. I asked them to underline each heading so it would be noticeable.

The title of Jacob's book was *Differences, Differences, Differences: Differences Between Grasshopper and Cricket*, and the page headings included "Antenna," "Legs," "Eyes," and "Body." Sarah's book was *The Book of the Five Senses*, and her page headings included "Senses on Your Face," "Dog's Senses," "Eyes," and "Tasting."

Day 5

On this day, the children gathered on the rug to write their tables of contents. Each brought their book pages, a pencil, a clipboard, and blank pieces of paper. As they worked, I demonstrated the procedure at the easel. First, they put the pages in the order they wanted and numbered each one. Then they wrote *Table of Contents* at the top of a blank sheet of paper, listed the page headings, and wrote the page numbers.

As they completed their tables of contents, some children returned to their seats to add more pages to their books, while others began working on their committee's displays and bulletin board presentations. A few were eager to return to the writing they had put aside to write their information book. Brandon went back to writing *My Trip to California*, which was up to about sixty-nine pages at that point. Eric got out his manuscript for a story about ants.

Day 6

Again we worked at the rug, this time to make indexes. Each child brought a clipboard, pencil, blank paper, and his or her table of contents. We looked at the index of *The Survival of Fish* and discussed that although the topics were in alphabetical order, there wasn't a topic for each of the twenty-six letters.

I used Alex's table of contents to demonstrate how to rearrange the topics in alphabetical order for the index. We said the alphabet until we came to a title that began with the letter. I wrote the topic, followed by the page number, on the easel, and we continued. When we came to two topics beginning with the same letter, I showed them how to go to the next letter and alphabetize using that one. Then the children began to work on their own, and I helped as needed.

I purposely kept this demonstration brief because I knew that the children needed to try it out on their own and would be most successful if they discovered their own system. Also, since I had never asked first graders to create their own indexes, I wasn't sure whether the task was too complicated for them. I decided that if they couldn't get involved in the process and do most of it independently, a long explanation from me wouldn't be of much value.

The children got right to work, conferring with each other and only occasionally asking for my help. When they shared their finished books with me later, I was surprised that almost everyone's index was in alphabetical order. When I asked them how they went about it, they were able to explain their own process. Andrew told me that he just said the alphabet and wrote down the words. Brandon explained that he just went to the next letter if the first letter was the same. Learning to alphabetize seemed so easy when it was done in an authentic context for a meaningful purpose.

Day 7

This was the last day we worked on our books as a group; everyone made a cover. We reviewed some of the important ideas about book covers, which we had discussed for another project, and then the children made a rough draft. As they finished their final cover, some added title, dedication, and "about the author" pages. Finally, they put their books in order and stapled them.

All the books were shared on the last visitors day of the year, when family and friends came to the class to celebrate the year's work.

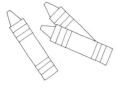

Welcome to the Waterworks

"Welcome to the Haynes School Waterworks" read the sign outside my classroom. The waterworks project was part of a schoolwide theme on water. It was generated by the students' intense enjoyment of and interest in *The Magic School Bus Goes to the Waterworks*, by Joanna Cole, which I had read to the class.

We made a model of the public water supply system, similar to the model in the book, to trace the path of water from reservoir to kitchen sink. The children could crawl through the model almost like the children in the book floated in their water bubble from the reservoir to the sink. Then, we invited our families and other classrooms to visit the waterworks.

Getting Started

To plan the project, students sat on the rug with clipboards, paper, and pencils, and took notes while I reread the story. On the top half of their paper, they wrote or drew pictures of materials we might need; on the bottom half, they drew plans of the model and wrote down things they wanted to be certain to include.

1. Big boxes
2. Cardboard
3. Cereal boxes
4. Pipes and tubes
5. Cotton balls
6. Sand and gravel
7. Water-testing kit
8. Chlorine box

FIGURE 1 *Materials needed for waterworks*

As we talked, I wrote my notes at the easel. Some of the children copied my list, others added their own notes to it, and a few drew pictures. The children discussed what they were writing and drawing with the people sitting near them.

I collected their papers and, after school, consolidated the ideas into two lists. The list that specified what to include in the project was posted in our room; the other, detailing materials we might need, was photocopied so that each child could take it home.

Group Decisions

Within a week, parents had supplied us with the boxes and other materials we needed to start construction. The class was divided into four groups, each named after a river (Amazon, Ganges, Mississippi, and Nile). Each group was responsible for constructing one of the main sections: the reservoir, the cleaning tank, the sand and gravel tank, and the holding tank.

With the help of parents, the children decorated the insides of the boxes. They drew pictures on and glued recycled materials (cotton balls, gravel, etc.) to the inside walls. They referred continually to *The Magic School Bus Goes to the Waterworks* while they worked on their model. This initial construction was not structured or defined by me because I wanted to see what ideas the children would develop. I felt they needed to plunge in and "have a go" in order to have better understanding of what we were doing.

At the end of the construction, we got together as a class, revisited the book, and looked at the sections as each group explained what it had done. Then we set up the boxes and everyone crawled through all the sections. Afterward we made some important decisions. We decided that to help visitors understand how water gets from the reservoir to the kitchen sink, we needed more pictures and written descriptions on the outside of the boxes to describe what was happening on the inside.

First, we covered each box with craft paper. Some children measured the length and width of the boxes with Unifix cubes and transferred the measurement to inches with a yardstick. Others helped glue the paper.

For the next few days, each group made pictures and additional signs for the outside of its section. We had spent a lot of time looking at the border illustrations in Lynne Cherry's *A River Ran Wild*, so we decided that our drawings would have a border, too.

We looked at several other books with borders and listed different border possibilities: information, labels, a story, patterns (relating to the topic or plain), and corner illustrations. I drew the border lines on each paper, and the children added a border of their choice. Then, we attached the four sections of the waterworks together.

The School Bus

We made the school bus from a long cardboard box that we covered with yellow craft paper and decorated with water motifs. This became the entrance to the waterworks.

In the book, as the children leave the bus, they float in bubbles on their journey from the reservoir through the waterworks. I asked the children to draw themselves inside bubbles that I had outlined on eight-and-a-half-by-eleven-inch white construction paper. My aide demonstrated ways to draw action figures to fill the space. She used children as models and related some of the shapes she drew to the shapes of letters. For example, she commented that the shape of Erica's arms when she crossed them reminded her of a *w*. The children got to work, first sketching with a pencil and then filling in their sketches with magic markers. They cut out the bubbles, and we hung them across the room to welcome guests to our classroom and to the waterworks.

Readers Theater

We decided to use readers theater to explain the waterworks to our visitors. I adapted material from *The Magic School Bus Goes to the Waterworks* to describe the four sections. I enlarged the text on the computer and pasted it on two big pieces of cardboard so the children could read their parts easily. Each child chose a sentence to read, and the whole group read the title, main headings, and extra lines together. The group monitor held up the page in the book that described the section we were reading about.

Sharing the Project

Throughout the project, we discussed ways of sharing the waterworks project with others. We decided to invite visitors—parents, foster parents, younger siblings, grandparents, relatives, friends, and anyone else the children wanted—to a twenty-minute group presentation.

As their visitors arrived, the children showed them around the room. At the appointed time, I started the tape "This Pretty Planet," composed and performed by Peter and Mary Alice Amidon, which was the signal for the children to bring their guests to the rug. We sang the first two songs from the tape, "This Pretty Planet" and "Water, Water Everywhere," both of which were written on charts for the children and visitors to follow.

I took a few minutes to welcome everyone, thank the visitors for their continued support, and tell them about this wonderful class, which now called itself "The Learning Class, the Thinking Class, the Singing Class, and the Caring Class." Then we presented the readers theater piece and ended by singing "I Like the Rivers," an innovation on Clyde Belanger's *I Like the Rain.*

The students were very enthusiastic, and they wanted to share our waterworks with the school, so we invited each classroom in which one of my students had a sibling. Some of the children wrote invitations that they delivered, and I arranged the times with the teachers so we could work around specialist schedules and lunch times.

We gave four performances, accommodating eight classes in all. We sang two songs from the tape, then performed the readers theater piece, and finally invited the children to imagine they were water bubbles being purified as they flowed from a reservoir to a kitchen sink.

Real world skills? You bet! Whole engagement? All the way!

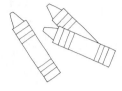

Visitors Day:
A Time to Shine

There's a crescendo of planning, participation, and engagement in my first grade four times a year—October, December, March, and June—as we get ready for visitors day. On visitors day the very important people in the children's lives visit the classroom, participate in a group time, and see what the children have been learning. The children invite these VIPs, who include parents, siblings not attending the school, aunts, uncles, grandparents, foster parents, other caregivers, and friends.

Although every visitors day follows the same general format, each one emphasizes something special. The one held in early October gives the children a chance to introduce their visitors to the daily classroom routine and gives me a chance to show family and friends what the children learn during shared literacy. The two visitors days held during the middle of the year each take place at the end of a theme study so that we can share what we've learned and demonstrate the progress we've made in reading, writing, and math. The last visitors day brings the year to an end through celebration and gives me an opportunity to thank the parents for their support.

The Best Time

I've found that the best time to have visitors in the classroom is between morning recess and lunch. That way, we have time to get ready in the morning, and the visitors are able to come to school during their lunch hour.

When the visitors arrive, they're shown around the room by the children until I start singing. That's the signal for everyone to come to the rug for group time. Group time lasts about twenty minutes, after which visitors time can continue exploring the room and leave whenever they're ready.

Getting Ready

The children and I start talking about visitors day several weeks ahead of time. We send the date and time home at least ten days in advance so the visitors can arrange their schedules.

We plan the group time and practice the songs and readings we will present. We also decide on the projects we want to share and the ongoing work, such as writing folders and math journals, we want visitors to see.

On the day before each visitors day, the children use clipboards, pencils, and paper to list the things in the classroom they want to be sure to show their visitors. (As is the case with all note taking and list making, children can draw pictures as well as write words. This is a great help to children who aren't writing conventionally, or who like to express themselves through drawing.)

We then share as a group on the rug, and I write the children's ideas on chart paper. The children are encouraged to add new ideas and correct those already noted in their clipboard lists.

On visitors day, the clipboards, along with other work such as projects and writing folders, are at the children's places, ready to be shown to the visitors.

October Visitors Day

I hold the first visitors day of the year four to six weeks after school starts. I announce it at the parent open house in September, and we send home an invitation the following week.

The focus of the October visitors day is on how teaching and learning happen in the classroom. We demonstrate the classroom routines, as well as the reading, writing, and math materials the children use. The children have listed many of the materials in their individual clipboard lists, and I've asked them to be sure to include writing folders and science observation papers. Since we use Cuisenaire rods extensively throughout the year, I put them out on a table.

During the group time the visitors attend, we have a shared reading lesson. We sing several songs and read a big book as I point. I ask the children what they notice. They may find specific letters, or mark off spaces between words, or suggest other words that would make sense in the text. We might reread a sentence to help figure out an unknown word, or predict and discuss what might come next in a story. We fill in the letters I have left out of the morning message.

This demonstration of shared reading is very important because it enables the visitors to see the merit and opportunities of learning as a community. It gives me a chance to demonstrate how children learn reading and writing skills and strategies in the context of whole texts, and shows the value and procedure of the explicit teaching I employ. During this time, I also make announcements, tell the children what a good job they are doing, and thank the parents for their support.

During their tour of the room, the visitors see the classroom materials and the children's work. This is especially important at the beginning of the year, since papers are not sent home daily. Visitors can also become familiar with some of the math materials we'll be using throughout the year. (The core of the math program involves manipulatives and small- and large-group problem solving.)

Visitors are told that they can come to the classroom at other times to look at the writing and science files, and that all of the children's work will be sent home at the end of the year.

Visitors are very interested in learning the daily classroom routine. They want to picture what the children do during their day in school. Understanding emerges as they sign in (just as the children do when they first enter the classroom), participate in shared reading, and complete their tour of the room.

December and March Visitors Days

These visitors days are each scheduled as part of the culmination of a theme study, and provide an authentic opportunity to share what we have been studying.

Since children's energy is very high in December, I always plan a theme study to channel this energy. The study ends with a visitors day a few days before vacation. The March visitors day is usually held before spring vacation, as we finish another study (which is often a part of a schoolwide theme).

During group time on these visitors days, some of the focus is on the theme we have been studying. I include songs and choral readings, and I demonstrate skills and strategies that the children are presently learning.

The children's clipboard lists include many of the items from previous visitors days, as well as new ones they think the visitors should see. Some items—have-a-go dictionaries and papers, math diaries, expanded observation forms, and reader-response journals, for example—are now an important part of the learning routine.

June Visitors Day

On the last visitors day of the school year, we celebrate our year together through song, review the work we have done all year, and say goodbye in a formal way. I try to schedule the day so that it takes place about one week before the final day of school.

This day requires a lot of preparation because we have to complete our main projects—our writing portfolios, reader-response journals, math diaries, and science folders. However, we then have the last few days to relax and be together, to finish saying goodbye, and to begin to dismantle the room.

During group time on the June visitors day, we sing some favorite songs, focusing on songs of peace as a way of expressing our classroom community. The children read the article they wrote for the end-of-the-year newspaper, and tell one thing that they learned in first grade. I thank the parents for their support, and tell them how the children have developed as readers, writers, and mathematicians.

At their places, the children display their clipboard lists, writing portfolios, math journals, science observation booklets, special learning projects, and copies of the class learning list and end-of-the-year newspaper. The visitors take these with them when they leave.

Summing It Up

Visitors days are beneficial to the children, the visitors, and me. As the children prepare for and participate in visitors days, they become increasingly engaged in the process and content of their learning, and I learn what the children value most in the classroom. The visitors have a chance to be involved in the children's life in school and to keep abreast of their progress throughout the year. I am given the opportunity to inform the visitors about the classroom and to speak individually with each of them. We all benefit from the closer communication that develops among us.

Resources

For Teachers

Avery, Carol. 1993. *And with a Light Touch: Learning About Reading, Writing, and Teaching with First Graders.* Portsmouth, NH: Heinemann.

Calkins, L. M. 1994. *The Art of Teaching Writing.* New ed. Portsmouth, NH: Heinemann.

Cambourne, B. 1988. *The Whole Story: Natural Learning and the Acquisition of Literacy in the Classroom.* New York: Ashton Scholastic.

Clay, M. 1993a. *An Observation Survey of Early Literacy Achievement.* Portsmouth, NH: Heinemann.

———. 1993b. *Reading Recovery: A Guidebook for Teachers in Training.* Portsmouth, NH: Heinemann.

———. 1991. *Becoming Literate: The Construction of Inner Control.* Portsmouth, NH: Heinemann.

Cochrane, O., D. Cochrane, S. Scalena & E. Buchanan. 1984. *Reading, Writing and Caring.* Katonah, NY: Richard C. Owen.

Cordeiro, P. 1995. *Endless Possibilities: Generating Curriculum in Social Studies and Literacy.* Portsmouth, NH: Heinemann.

Fisher, B. 1995. *Thinking and Learning Together: Curriculum and Community in a Primary Classroom.* Portsmouth, NH: Heinemann.

———. 1994. *Classroom Close-Up, Bobbi Fisher: Organization and Management.* Bothell, WA: The Wright Group. Videotape.

————. 1991. *Joyful Learning: A Whole Language Kindergarten.* Portsmouth, NH: Heinemann.

————. 1990. "Children as Authorities on Their Own Reading." In *Workshop 2: Beyond the Basal,* edited by Nancie Atwell. Portsmouth, NH: Heinemann.

Goodman, K. 1993. *Phonics Phacts.* Portsmouth, NH: Heinemann.

————. 1986. *What's Whole in Whole Language?* Portsmouth, NH: Heinemann.

Goodman, Y. 1978. "Kidwatching: An Alternative to Testing." *Journal of National Elementary School Principals* 57(4):22–27.

Goodman, Y., D. Watson, & C. Burke. 1984. *Reading Miscue Inventory: Alternative Procedures.* Katonah, NY: Richard C. Owen.

Graves, D. 1994. *A Fresh Look at Writing.* Portsmouth, NH: Heinemann.

————. 1991. *Build a Literate Classroom.* Portsmouth, NH: Heinemann.

————. 1984. "The Enemy Is Orthodoxy." In *A Researcher Learns to Write.* Portsmouth, NH: Heinemann.

Hansen, J. & D. Graves. 1983. "The Author's Chair," *Language Arts* 60:176–83.

Holdaway, D. 1979. *The Foundations of Literacy.* Portsmouth, NH: Heinemann.

Katz, L. & S. Chard. 1989. *Engaging Children's Minds: The Project Approach.* Norwood, NJ: Ablex.

Mills, H., T. O'Keefe & D. Stephens. 1992. *Looking Closely: Exploring the Role of Phonics in One Whole Language Classroom.* Urbana, IL: National Council of Teachers of English.

Mills, H., T. O'Keefe & D. Whitin. 1996. *Mathematics in the Making.* Portsmouth, NH: Heinemann.

Murray, D. 1989. *Expecting the Unexpected: Teaching Myself—and Others—to Read and Write.* Portsmouth, NH: Heinemann.

Ostrow, J. 1995. *A Room with a Different View: First Through Third Graders Build Community and Create Curriculum.* York, ME: Stenhouse.

Routman, R. 1991. *Invitations: Changing as Teachers and Learners K–12.* Portsmouth, NH: Heinemann.

Peterson, R. 1992. *Life in a Crowded Place.* Portsmouth, NH: Heinemann.

Seigle, P. & G. Macklem. 1993. *Reach Out to Schools: Social Competency Program.* Wellesley, MA: The Stone Center, Wellesley College.

Smith, F. 1988. *Joining the Literacy Club: Further Essays into Education*. Portsmouth, NH: Heinemann.

Tompkins, G. E. & L. M. McGee.1993. *Teaching Reading with Literature*. New York: Macmillan.

Weaver, C. 1994. *Reading Process and Practice: From Socio-psycholinguistics to Whole Language*. 2d ed. Portsmouth, N.H.: Heinemann.

————. 1990. *Understanding Whole Language: From Principles to Practice*. Portsmouth, NY: Heinemann.

Wellington (New Zealand) Department of Education. 1985. *Reading in Junior Classes*. Katonah, NY: Richard C. Owen.

Vygotsky, L. 1978. *Mind in Society: The Development of Higher Psychological Processes*. Cambridge, MA: Harvard University Press.

For Children

Amidon, P. & M. Amidon. *This Pretty Planet*. Audiocassette. (Order address: 8 Willow Street, Brattleboro, VT 05301.)

Belanger, C. 1988. *I Like the Rain*. Crystal Lake, IL: Rigby. Audiocassette and big book.

Biddulph, F. & J. Biddulph. 1993. *The Survival of Fish* . Bothell, WA: The Wright Group.

Cherry, L. 1992. *A River Ran Wild*. New York: Harcourt Brace.

Chapin, T. *Family Tree*. Sundance Music, Inc. Audiocassette. (Distributed by A & M Records, Inc.)

Charette, R. *Popcorn and Other Songs to Munch On*. Pine Point Records. Audiocassette. (Order address: North Windham, ME 04062.)

Cole, J. 1986. *The Magic School Bus at the Waterworks*. New York: Scholastic.

Cowley, J. 1980. *In a Dark, Dark Wood*. Bothell, WA: The Wright Group.

————. 1990. *Mrs. Wishy-Washy*. Bothell, WA: The Wright Group.

Drew, D. 1988. *Somewhere in the Universe*. Crystal Lake, IL: Rigby.

Gentner, N. 1993. *Gravity*. Bothell, WA: The Wright Group. Audiocassette and big book.

Grammer, R. & K. Grammer. 1986. *Teaching Peace*. Smilin' Atcha Music. Audiocassette.

Grater, M. 1988. *On Sunday the Giant* . . . Bothell, WA: The Wright Group.

Lehr, Lore. 1970. *A Letter Goes to Sea*. Irvington-on-Hudson, NY: Harvey House.

Literacy 2000. Series. Crystal Lake, IL: Rigby.

McDermott, G. 1974. *Arrow to the Sun*. New York:Viking.

Martin, B., Jr. 1983. *Brown Bear, Brown Bear*. New York: Holt, Rinehart & Winston.

Nellie Edge Resources, P.O. Box 12399, Salem, OR. 97309. Big books.

Parks, B., & J. Smith. *The Enormous Watermelon*. Crystal Lake, IL: Rigby.

Peek, M. 1985. *Mary Wore Her Red Dress*. New York: Clarion.

Raffi. 1992. *Baby Beluga: Songs to Read*. New York: Crown.

Story Box. Series. Bothell, WA: The Wright Group.

Sunshine Books. Series. Bothell, WA: The Wright Group.

Twig Books. Series. Bothell, WA: The Wright Group.

Van Allsburg, C. 1988. *Two Bad Ants*. New York: Houghton Mifflin.

Page 1. "The Environment Reflects the Program." Reprinted with the permission of the publisher, *Teaching K–8*, from the September 1989 issue of *Teaching K–8* magazine.

Page 6. "Reading and Writing in a Kindergarten Classroom." Reprinted with the permission of the ERIC Digest. This article originally appeared as an ERIC/REC publication and can be found in the ERIC database as ED331030.

Page 10. "Getting Started with Writing." Reprinted with the permission of the publisher, *Teaching K–8*, from the September 1991 issue of *Teaching K–8* magazine.

Page 14. "Demonstrations and Minilessons." Reprinted with the permission of the publisher, *Teaching K–8*, from the October 1991 issue of *Teaching K–8* magazine.

Page 17. "Sitting in the Author's Chair." Reprinted with the permission of the publisher, *Teaching K–8*, from the November 1991 issue of *Teaching K–8* magazine.

Page 20. "Beyond Letter of the Week." Reprinted with the permission of the publisher, *Teaching K–8*, from the January 1996 issue of *Teaching K–8* magazine.

Page 24. "Assessing Emergent and Initial Readers." Reprinted with the permission of the publisher, *Teaching K–8*, from the November 1989 issue of *Teaching K–8* magazine.

Page 28. "Starting the Year in a First-Grade Classroom." Reprinted with the permission of the publisher, *Teaching K–8*, from the September 1992 issue of *Teaching K–8* magazine.

Page 32. "Planning for the First Day of School." Reprinted with the permission of the publisher, *Teaching K–8*, from the September 1993 issue of *Teaching K–8* magazine.

Page 37. "Getting Democracy into First Grade—or Any Grade." Reprinted with the permission of the publisher, *Teaching K–8*, from the September 1994 issue of *Teaching K–8* magazine.

Page 42. "Supporting Reading Development in a First-Grade Classroom." Reprinted with the permission of the publisher, *Teaching K–8*, from the November 1992 issue of *Teaching K–8* magazine.

Page 46. "Trusting Individual Readers." Reprinted with the permission of the publisher, *The Colorado Communicator*, from the June 1992 issue, Volume 15, Number 3, pp. 8-10 of *The Colorado Communicator*.

Page 50. "We *Do* Teach Phonics." Reprinted with the permission of the publisher, *Teaching K–8*, from the September 1995 issue of *Teaching K–8* magazine.

Page 54. "Writing Workshop in a First-Grade Classroom." Reprinted with the permission of the publisher, *Teaching K–8*, from the October 1995 issue of *Teaching K–8* magazine.

Page 59. "Questions and Answers About Spelling." Reprinted with the permission of the Greater Boston Council of the International Reading Association. This article first appeared as "Teacher to Teacher: Spelling in the Classroom" in the Greater Boston Council Newsletter.

Page 61. "Children as Authorities on Their Own Writing." Reprinted with the permission of the publisher, *Writing Teacher*, from the May 1993 issue of *Writing Teacher* magazine.

Page 69. "Workshop Time: Generating Curriculum." Reprinted with the permission of the publisher, *Teaching K–8*, from the October 1994 issue of *Teaching K–8* magazine.

Page 74. "Writing Information Books in First Grade." Reprinted with the permission of the publisher, *Teaching K–8*, from the November 1994 issue of *Teaching K–8* magazine.

Page 78. "Welcome to the Waterworks." Reprinted with the permission of the publisher, *Teaching K–8*, from the October 1993 issue of *Teaching K–8* magazine.

Page 82. "Visitors Day: A Time to Shine." Reprinted with the permission of the publisher, *Teaching K–8*, from November 1993 issue of *Teaching K–8* magazine.